PREPARING FOR PEACE

Syracuse Studies on Peace and Conflict Resolution
Harriet Hyman Alonso, Charles Chatfield, and Louis Kriesberg
Series Editors

Preparing for Peace

Conflict Transformation
Across Cultures

John Paul Lederach

SYRACUSE UNIVERSITY PRESS

The paper used in this publication meets the minimum requirements of American National Standard for Information Sciences—Permanence of Paper for Printed
Library Materials, ANSI Z39.48–1984. ∞™

Library of Congress Cataloging-in-Publication Data
Lederach, John Paul.
Preparing for Peace : conflict transformation across cultures /
John Paul Lederach.
p.   cm. — (Syracuse studies on peace and conflict resolution)
Includes bibliographical references and index.
ISBN 0-8156-2656-8 (cloth : acid-free)
ISBN 0-8156-2725-4 (pbk.: alk. paper)
1. International relations and culture.   2. Pacific settlement of
international disputes.   I. Title.   II. Series
JX1255.L43 1995
337—dc20   94-49199

Manufactured in the United States of America

To Angie and Josh,
who have taught me much about the joy of living
and the excitement of discovery.

John Paul Lederach is professor of sociology and conflict studies at Eastern Mennonite University and director of the International Conciliation Service of the Mennonite Central Committee. He has traveled worldwide as a mediation trainer and conflict resolution specialist and is the author of numerous books.

Contents

Figures

Acknowledgments

This book has been a long time in the making. It owes its ideas and experiences to a long list of people through the Americas, Africa, Asia, and Europe. To the many people who have participated with me in workshops and training seminars I am deeply indebted. More specifically on this final draft I would like to acknowledge the very helpful comments from Dr. Christopher Moore, Dr. Dianne LeResche, and Dr. Louis Kriesberg. I could not possibly have met my final deadline without the logistical support of Cheryl Helmuth and the careful proofreading help from my mother Naomi Lederach.

The first draft of this book was in the form of a paper and research conducted with the Institute for Peace and Conflict Studies at Conrad Grebel College, through a grant provided by the Inter-racial and Cross-cultural Conflict Resolution Project with the financial support of the Ontario Anti-Racism Secretariat. I am especially grateful to Dean Peachy for his assistance, suggestions, and encouragement in the early stages.

Harrisonburg, Virginia   John Paul Lederach
May 1994

PART ONE

The Training Project in Perspective

1

Introduction

The dusty road seemed to go on forever. Outside of Panama City the macadam became gravel, and the gravel mostly dust, rivets, and potholes in the middle of dry season as we made our way to Yaviza, the remote town near the Colombian border. There, some six hours out of the capital, the highway ends and travel begins by canoe, horse, or foot.

My heart jumped as we entered the school compound at the edge of Yaviza where I was to give a week-long training seminar on conflict resolution to leaders of the indigenous Wounaan and Embere communities. The participants of the seminar came out to greet the arrival of our pickup, some of them having come from as far away as two days' travel by canoe. Looking back at my journal entry, I remember a feeling of anxiety and challenge paralleled by the words of Father Niall O'Brien (1987) in the opening lines of the book on his Asian experience. "I thought again," he wrote, "how presumptuous I had been in coming to the Philippines thinking only to teach. The truth was most of the time I was the one learning. . . . "

"What does a North American have to teach these people about conflict resolution?" I wrote that evening. "How can this training event be relevant and useful in their context?" Hundreds of hours of seminars and training events later—with very diverse

groups across Latin America, Africa, South East Asia, and
Europe—those questions still remain. The tentative and emerging
answers have produced some significant changes in how I think
about and approach conflict resolution "training" across cultures,
changes that lie at the root of this book.

There has been an interest for some time in the issue of culture and negotiation, particularly as related to international busi-
ness and diplomacy (Iklé 1964; Fisher 1980; Cohen 1991). These
have concentrated on outlining key differences in cultural values
and orientations, and how those impact specific negotiations
across cultures, often comparing two cultures described in broad
macro terms. Nader and Todd (1978) and Gulliver (1979) provided
early empirical studies of cross-cultural dispute resolution, from
the perspective of law systems, articulating both the variety of
approaches and identifying important commonalities.

As Duryea's (1992) recent comprehensive literature review
suggests, it is with the growth of alternative dispute resolution
and mediation applications in North America that the relationship
of culture and conflict has become an increasingly debated topic.
Culture has become, as Wally Warfield put it, "the new sexy issue" in the field of dispute resolution. This concern in conflict resolution coincides generally with the rising interest in parallel fields
of intercultural education, multiculturalism, and even
transcultural medical care and counseling (Duryea 1992). In the
field of conflict resolution, we see more research and conferences
emerging with culture and diversity as the central theme. Some
efforts concentrate on specific groups and how they handle conflict, as seen in LeResche's work on Korean Americans (1990),
Dator's work on the dispute processes in Hawaii (1991), or
Cohen's volume on the cultural aspects of the Israeli-Egyptian conflict (1990). Others, like Augsburger's (1991) recent volume on
mediation, have put their energies toward identifying broad cross-
cultural comparisons.

I personally have experienced an increased number of re-
quests for what many refer to as "cross-cultural training," particularly in the mediation field. In almost every case, I have
experienced an inner tension, a struggle between how to respond
appropriately to their interests and concerns and do justice to

the depth and breadth of the issue. Increasingly, I believe my inner tension emerges from the assumptions that surround our understanding of and approach to culture in dispute resolution, assumptions that rarely make explicit fundamental concerns about cultural appropriateness, dominance, and ideology that underlie the meaning and purpose of training and the expansion of the field.

These difficult questions keep cropping up for me. What are we up to when we incorporate cultural concerns in our training? What do we mean by "culture" and how is it addressed? Who are we concerned about? What ultimately are our goals? Whose interests are served, both latent and direct, when culture enters the field of conflict resolution? How does the way we approach training impact our projected goals? These questions suggest that culture is more than an additional skill or technique and training is more than a neutral and benign tool used in the simple dissemination of a good thing. It is a project worthy of exploration and constructive critique.

Purpose and Outline

Although the fields of conflict resolution and mediation have grown and expanded, and the interest in applications across and in multicultural settings has heightened, little has been written about the function or methodology of training in these practices, except in manuals and other training materials. Through this essay, I intend to open a constructive dialogue on the purpose and practice of training in conflict resolution and, more specifically, mediation, particularly as these fields have expanded from a mainstream North American base and have pushed across cultural, ethnic, and national boundaries.

Three largely implicit premises seem to dominate the mainstream dispute resolution view of training about culture. First, we appear to operate with the basic assumption that the model we use in one setting is sufficiently universal to use with "adjustments" and "sensitivity" in others (Folberg and Taylor 1984). That is, we take a high view of transferability of conflict resolution skills and processes. Second, we seem to assume that culture is an aspect of conflict resolution that can be reduced to technique, essentially through raising the level of sensitivity and skill of practitioners. Third, and a logical consequence of the technique orientation, much of what we do in terms of cultural training is aimed at empowering the professional and increasing the competence of the already trained. Thus we find that culture is most often included in advanced training (Duryea 1992). Each of these assumptions circles back to my questions and inner tension.

My fundamental thesis is that we need to explore critically at a much deeper level both the content and the approach to conflict resolution training and its relationship to culture. I believe this is more readily accomplished if we move beyond the rhetoric of dispute resolution training, and what it purports to do, to a critical examination of training as a project, a socially constructed, educational phenomenon comprised of purpose, process, and content and inherently encompassing culture and ideology.

Stated bluntly, conflict resolution training in the dominant North American culture represents among other things the packaging, presentation, and selling of social knowledge. Whose knowledge, under what package, delivered through what mechanism, and received by what populations are all legitimate and necessary questions for investigation and study if we are to achieve a critical understanding of the training project. By critical I do not mean an exercise of finding fault or finger-pointing. I do refer to a careful and judicious evaluation of our activities with an eye toward improvement and a call for both creativity and consistency with the values espoused in this field.

This essay does not emerge from rigorous scientific research or a survey of training practices, although it draws from a number of studies and recent surveys (LeResche and Spruill 1991; Duryea 1992). Rather it is an inductive effort, rooted in personal experiences and in experiments with direct training across cultures, and aimed at presenting a theoretical and a practical framework related to training and culture. I will develop in three sections this framework, which does not pretend to be more than a contribution to the ongoing growth and maturation of the field.

In the first section, I explore whether our approach to training in conflict resolution is consistent with the goals we espouse in the field—an exploration that becomes more readily apparent and crucial as we cross culture and class lines. Given both the critique of training and the models I will describe, I believe it is crucial to clarify how I understand the ultimate goals, purpose, and values that underlie conflict resolution. Further, I will draw some broad lessons from the fields of popular education, appropriate technology, and ethnography as useful alternative and conceptual bases for any pedagogical project. I include these additional fields as important theoretical frames of reference aimed at expanding a too-often narrow technical view of our field in terms of training.

In the second section, for analytical purposes, I will develop a spectrum of training models suggesting two major types: the prescriptive approach based on transferring conflict resolution technology from one setting to another, and the elicitive approach based on building from cultural resources in a given setting. The models are developed to provide us with a tool for comparison and to explore the shift in emphasis and thinking inherent in an elicitive-oriented point of view as it relates to goals of conflict transformation.

In the final section, I will describe in more detail my own experiments and experiences with the elicitive model, demonstrating at a practical level how elicitive-oriented training can be carried out based on a sampling of specific approaches and exercises that illustrate the shift in thinking and practice. I will also extrapolate from the elicitive framework some ideas about application in multicultural settings.

My purpose in these three sections is to develop both a broad theoretical and analytical view of conflict resolution training and to then explore the practical, experiential side of how that framework is applied. Throughout, we will be dealing with the key concepts of conflict and culture. It will be useful, therefore, to briefly outline, as a conclusion to this introductory chapter, my working assumptions in regard to these concepts.

Assumptions on Culture and Conflict

An old Hasidic saying has it that humans were created because God liked to tell stories. I once heard a revision suggesting that humans were created because God liked to hear stories. A third variation makes note that we humans are storytellers, and that we live in the peculiar paradox of being the authors of the stories we experience as real. All three versions lead to the assumptions I bring to culture and conflict, for each points to the social construction of human experience, interaction, and social realities.

A social constructionist view of conflict builds on an important body of literature in the social sciences, although these authors tend not to be frequently cited in conflict resolution literature. For example, phenomenologist Alfred Schutz (1967) or symbolic interactionist Herbert Blumer (1969) provide us with important perspectives and lenses on social interaction but are not viewed per se as conflict theorists. However, their theoretical frameworks are crucial for developing a social constructionist understanding of conflict. At essence, their approaches suggest the construction of social meaning, as an intersubjective process, lies at the heart of how human conflict is created. Such an approach contrasts but does not necessarily contradict other explanations of social conflict. For example, the conflict functionalism of both Simmel (1955) and, subsequently, Coser (1956) undertook the study of human disputes from the perspective of its role in maintaining and changing social groups. Others have concentrated on the communicative patterns and dynamics of conflict, concentrating on the micro-episodes and structure of interpersonal exchange (Hocker and Wilmot 1991). At the opposite end, Marx as a social theorist, delineated a macro view of conflict based on the concept of historical materialism and the struggle of classes, which posits economic structure and control of the means of production as the primary determinants of social conflict (McLellan 1977).

The point of departure for the social constructionist view, however, is the fundamental idea that social conflict emerges and develops on the basis of the meaning and interpretation people involved attach to action and events. Social meaning is lodged in the accumulated knowledge, or what Schutz (1967) calls a person's "bank of knowledge." From this starting point, conflict is connected to meaning, meaning to knowledge, and knowledge is rooted in culture.

We must be careful not to push a single theoretical approach as the only mechanism for understanding social conflict. Experience, particularly from a practitioner's view, suggests the need for multidisciplinary perspectives (Moore 1986). However, in exploring the questions of culture and training, which I suggest is the packaging of social knowledge, a theoretical approach that places primary emphasis on the construction of meaning and the role of knowledge is especially justified. Although my assumptions about conflict and culture may seem to be quite self-evident in some respects, I believe it is helpful to clarify the basic working assumptions of a constructionist view that underlies much of the perspective I will develop in this book.

✓ 1. I understand social conflict to be a natural, common experience present in all relationships and cultures.

✓ 2. I understand conflict to be a socially constructed cultural event. Conflicts do not "just happen" to people, people are active participants in creating situations and interactions they experience as conflict. This is the essential dialectic experienced in the construction of any social reality, as was well articulated by Schutz (1971) and Berger and Luckman (1967).

3. Conflict emerges through an interactive process based on the search for and creation of shared meaning.

4. The interactive process is accomplished through and rooted in people's perceptions, interpretations, expressions, and intentions, each of which grows from and cycles back to their common sense knowledge.

5. Meaning occurs as people locate themselves and social "things" such as situations, events, and actions in their accumulated knowledge. Meaning emerges by connecting one thing to another, by an act of comparison (Schutz 1971). Thus an important working assumption from this perspective is the idea that a person's common sense and accumulated experience and knowledge are the primary basis of how they create, understand, and respond to conflict.

6. I understand culture to be rooted in the shared knowledge and schemes created and used by a set of people for perceiving, interpreting, expressing, and responding to social realities around them.

(7.) I therefore assume that understanding the connection of social conflict and culture is not merely a question of sensitivity or of awareness, but a far more profound adventure of discovering and digging in the archeology of accumulated shared knowledge common to a set of people.

To summarize, a constructionist view suggests that people act on the basis of the meaning things have for them. Meaning is created through shared and accumulated knowledge. People from different cultural settings have developed many ways of creating and expressing as well as interpreting and handling conflict. A fundamental argument of this book is that understanding conflict and developing appropriate models of handling it will necessarily be rooted in, and must respect and draw from, the cultural knowledge of a people.

These assumptions come together in the form of a basic proposal we will explore in this essay. I suggest that training for conflict transformation and mediation must envision cultural knowledge as a key resource in both the creation and development of models appropriate to a given setting. In the following chapters, I will approach this idea through my lenses as a practitioner of cross-cultural and multicultural conflict resolution and mediation training, although much of what is articulated will be of direct interest to researchers and academics in the field. My experience suggests that we have not adequately probed the deeper questions about training methodology and purpose as we move in very diverse settings. To pursue this exploration, my approach will necessarily pose a certain polemic and critique, one that hopefully can contribute constructively to this field and the important goals and purposes that undergird its expansion.

2

A Framework for Building Peace

I t seems that the sociological laws of conflict are played out in predictable fashion regardless of the field, discipline, or people involved. Peacemakers are no exception. Over the years, I have moved in two broad camps, that of nonviolent social change, the "revolutionary" camp, and that of mediation, the "resolutionary" camp. I am always keenly interested in the language that dominates peoples' understandings, self-definitions, and experiences. I have noticed that these two camps have developed ways of describing self and others that create a certain tension through which we "peacemakers" attempt to separate and purify our respective groups.

This was summarized nicely in a recent conversation with a mediator friend who asked rhetorically, "You know the trouble with the activists?" and answered, "They assume that having the vision and speaking out for nonviolent social change is the same as having the technique and skill to."

"On the other side of the coin," I responded, "having the technique and skill does not necessarily provide the vision."

This exchange raises two key questions related to the conflict resolution field generally: Where we are going? And what are we up to? It insinuates a third question more specific to the subject matter of this book: How do our training practices relate to our

11

ultimate goals and purpose? Intrinsic to any training project are numerous assumptions about purpose and goals. Thus, before looking analytically at the training project, I believe it useful to be explicit about my view of the ultimate purpose and goals of the field into which the training endeavor fits.

In my view, the answers to the questions "where?" and "what?" start with the construction of a broader understanding and approach to building peace. Such a framework must be inclusive—embracing multiple facets, the interdependence of roles and activities, and a clear vision of the broader agenda peacemaking and conflict resolution efforts undertake. I suggest that three conceptual and practical pillars undergird this framework and delineate more clearly the purpose and goals in this field: the development of a long-term view of conflict; an adequate descriptive language; and an understanding of the value paradoxes in the peacemaking endeavor.

The Long View of Conflict

As a starting point, I wish to build on an early conceptual piece proposed by Quaker conciliator Adam Curle in his book *Making Peace* (1971). He suggests that the movement from unpeaceful to peaceful relationships can be charted in a matrix comparing levels of power with levels of awareness of conflicting interests and needs (see figure 1). The matrix is useful for plotting where we are in a given conflict and for suggesting potential activities we might choose to undertake at a given time. At least three key peacemaking functions identified in this progression toward change are education, advocacy, and mediation.

The roles emerge as we follow a typical path of conflict. According to Curle, education, or conscientization, is needed when the conflict is hidden and people are unaware of imbalances and injustices. This role is aimed at erasing ignorance and raising awareness as to the nature of unequal relationships and the need for addressing and restoring equity, as seen, of course, from the view of those experiencing the injustices.

Increased awareness of issues, needs, and interests leads to demands for changing the situation. Such demands are rarely

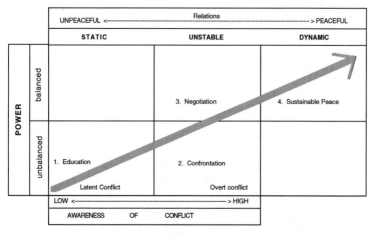

Figure 1
The Progression of Conflict
(Based on Curle 1971 and used with permission)

attained immediately and, more likely, are not even heard nor
taken seriously by those benefitting from the situation, who prefer to keep things as they are. Hence, the entry of advocates, who
work with and support those pursuing change. Their work pushes
for a balancing of power, that is, a recognition of mutual dependence increasing the voice of the less powerful and a legitimation
of their concerns. This happens through some form of confrontation involving choices between violent or nonviolent mechanisms
or a combination of both.

If successful, the confrontation will increase the awareness
of interdependence and balance power. Negotiation now becomes possible, and the role of mediation emerges. In essence,
negotiation means that the various people or groups involved
recognize they cannot simply impose their will or eliminate the
other side, but rather must work with each other to achieve their
goals.

Successful negotiations and mediation lead to a restructuring
of the relationship and deal with fundamental substantive and

procedural concerns. This result is what Curle refers to as increased justice or more peaceful relations. Obviously, at any point the path of conflict can jump or even circulate between several of the quadrants for extensive periods of time. For example, negotiations do not always (in fact may rarely) lead to restructured relationships. Confrontation does not automatically end in negotiation. But for our purposes here, we are interested in this progression as laying out a paradigm for a long-term view of conflict, one that contemplates both a vision of where we are going and a multiplicity of activities to get us there. We note several key ideas emerging from Curle's approach.

First, the framework suggests that education, advocacy, and mediation share the goal of change and restructuring unpeaceful relationships (see figure 2). They share the vision of justice, of substantive and procedural change. When justice ceases to be the goal, any particular role, activity, or strategy must be questioned. Where any approach is used as a ploy to co-opt or manipulate the less powerful and disadvantaged, it should not be pursued. It should be noted that Curle's overall scheme, while descriptive in nature, also assumes a value orientation in favor of less powerful groups attaining a voice if peaceful relations and restructuring are desired outcomes—an orientation I believe is the foundation for peacemaking endeavors.

Second, we note that these peacemaking activities overlap, complement, and, more importantly, are mutually supportive and dependent. Negotiation becomes possible when the needs and interests of all those involved and affected by the conflict are legitimated and articulated. This process happens most often through confrontation and advocacy that emerge from an awareness of the basic needs and interests. On the other hand, restructuring the relationship toward increased equality and justice does not emanate automatically from confrontation, unless we assume the total elimination of one side. Mediation can and should facilitate the articulation of legitimate needs and interests of all concerned into fair, practical, and mutually acceptable solutions.

It is worth noting where these roles differ. Advocacy, for example, chooses to stand by one side for justice's sake. Mediation chooses to stand in connection to all sides for justice's sake. Non-

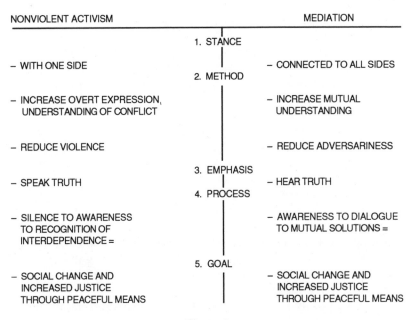

Figure 2

Conflict Transformation: A Comparison

violent advocacy, given the circumstances, pursues confrontation
by moving to produce and increase the overt expression of conflict, while seeking to reduce violence. Through conflict it seeks
to move from silence and complacency to awareness and change.
Mediation, building on the acute awareness of conflict, moves to
produce and increase mutual understanding while reducing
adversariness.

What is descriptively interesting is that the former is experienced as increasing conflict and the latter as reducing conflict,
creating the impression of incompatibility. This framework, however, suggests the inverse: that the longer-term progression of
conflict toward increased justice and peaceful relations must integrate and view these activities as necessary and mutually interdependent in the pursuit of just change and peaceful
transformation.

Pursuing an Adequate Language

Terminology that dominates a field or discipline evolves with the changing conceptual processes of its practitioners. Such is the case particularly in the area of conflict resolution. Resolution was an early and still dominant concept describing the more academic field of study and its practical application. The concept indicated a need to understand how conflict evolves and ends. It encouraged the development of strategies and skills for dealing with the volatile and too-often destructive outcomes of conflict. At times, however, resolution may conceptually and subtly promote the impression that conflict is undesirable and should be eliminated or at least reduced. Legitimate questions are raised about whether we really resolve a conflict or whether in many instances that is a desirable goal. Nader (1990 and 1993) has argued rather persuasively that the conflict resolution field has taken this lightly, where resolution too often has meant seeking to stop the conflict and create harmony at the expense of justice.

It is certainly true that in any conflict progression specific decisions are made and expressions of conflict may end. But if there is an ongoing relationship, conflict remains. If change increasing justice has not occurred because the root structural causes of conflict remain untouched, then reducing or eliminating the overt expression of the conflict may be an exercise of co-optation. Thus, as a concept, resolution may not adequately describe the ongoing nature of conflict in the relational ebb and flow over time, or its usefulness in the construction of peace, and sometimes inappropriately pushes for the premature reduction of confrontation.

Some years ago, conflict management entered practitioner parlance (Thomas 1976; Wehr 1979). Heavily Western in conception, management pointed toward the idea that conflict follows certain predictable patterns and dynamics that could be understood and regulated. As in building a bridge over a raging river, or damming it up to produce electricity, we could channel conflict energy toward productive outcomes. The evolving concept was an effort to take account of the nature and role of conflict in relationships; it was natural and should be managed. Management as a concept recognized that conflict was not resolved in the sense of getting rid of it, but rather emphasis was placed on affecting the destructive consequences and components.

Experience tells us, however, that we do not really manage human action and interaction in ways we might manage things in the physical world. Further, it raises the question of whether our primary interest in peacemaking is to reduce or control volatility. At a conceptual level, management provided a useful handle in the professionalization of the field and in carving a legitimate niche among other helping professions, but may not have clearly articulated the goals and purpose of justice and change. Hence, management does not capture the broader sense of peacemaking, as it narrows its focus to the technical and practical side of the effort.

Over the past years the idea of conflict transformation has emerged in the search for an adequate language to describe the peacemaking venture (Curle 1991, Kriesberg 1989, Ruppesinghe 1994). Transformation provides a more holistic understanding, which can be fleshed out at several levels. Unlike resolution and management, the idea of transformation does not suggest we simply eliminate or control conflict, but rather points descriptively toward its inherent dialectic nature. Social conflict is a phenomenon of human creation, lodged naturally in relationships. It is a phenomenon that transforms events, the relationships in which conflict occurs, and indeed its very creators. It is a necessary element in transformative human construction and reconstruction of social organization and realities. As such, transformation more closely acknowledges what social scientists have been suggesting for some time about the role and dynamics of social conflict: it moves through certain predictable phases transforming relationships and social organization (Coleman 1956; Boulding 1962).

Consider for a moment how social conflict transforms. For example, conflict changes communication patterns, affecting relationships and social organization. Typically, at times of increased tension there is less direct exchange between those experiencing the conflict and increased indirect communication by which others are brought in, changing the primary relationship and the broader social context in which the conflict occurs. This was one of the key findings early on by Coleman's (1956) study of community conflict and lies at the heart of how family systems approaches describe the impact of conflict (Friedman 1990). The chosen expression of conflict can transform not only the social organization but the very context. Moving from words to guns, from verbal disagreement to antagonism to overt mutually destructive hostility—these are expressive conflict transformations that produce polarization via reorganization of social alliances, separation, and changed goals.

Conflict also transforms perceptions, of self, others, and the issues in question, usually with the consequence of less accurate understanding of the other's intention and decreased ability to clearly articulate one's own intentions. This consequence relates to the psychological dimensions of conflict. In every instance it raises a question about self-identity and esteem. Volkan (1990) and Kelman (1965) suggest these elements are crucial, for example, in exploring and dealing with deep-rooted, protracted conflict where nearly institutionalized images of the enemy prevail and dominate perceptions.

However, transformation also suggests a *prescriptive* direction based on the core elements outlined in early developments in the field. Specifically, there is the idea that conflict unabated can take destructive patterns that should be channeled toward constructive expression. On the one hand, a transformation is assumed in terms of the relationship, which shifts from mutually destructive, unstable, and harmful expressions toward a mutually beneficial and cooperative basis. On the other hand, a transformation of the system and structure is assumed, in which the relationships are embedded and which can be changed by building on the energy and impact of conflict itself. In other words, conflict is seen as a transforming agent for systemic change.

In sum, transformation as a concept is both descriptive of the conflict dynamics and prescriptive of the overall purpose that building peace pursues, both in terms of changing destructive relationship patterns and in seeking systemic change. Transformation provides a language that more adequately approximates the nature of conflict and how it works and underscores the goals and purpose of the field. It encompasses a view that legitimizes conflict as an agent of change in relationships. It describes more accurately the impact of conflict on the patterns of communication,

expression, and perception. Transformation suggests a dynamic
understanding that conflict can move in destructive or constructive directions, but proposes an effort to maximize the achieve-
ment of constructive, mutually beneficial processes and outcomes.

Understanding the Paradoxical Values of Peacemaking

Approaching conflict from a dialectic perspective encourages
us to look at peacemaking in terms of paradoxes. A paradox is the
interplay of two opposite ideas or energies that seem to create an
irreconcilable contradiction. The irreconcilable nature emerges from
a tendency to understand contrary ideas in an either/or frame of
reference in which one must be chosen over the other. A paradoxical approach suggests the energy of the ideas is enhanced if they
are held together, like two sides of the coin (Smith and Berg 1987).
I have found the paradox a useful tool in understanding conflict
and in exploring the key values of peacemaking. I would suggest
at least four paradoxes, related to fundamental values in the peacemaking venture, whose potential energy is enormous if both concerns creating these paradoxes are embraced. I have tagged these
by various names for my own recollection and use.

The Freire Folly: Personal and Systemic Change

In the peacemaking endeavor, there seems to be a certain tension around how to pursue social change, which too often is posed
as an either/or contradiction: Is social change fundamentally a
process of personal or systemic transformation?

Paulo Freire, whose seminal work on pedagogy will inform numerous aspects of this book, suggests we understand social change
as including both. I have found it useful to step back and look at the
big picture related to Freire's pedagogical framework. In *Pedagogy of
the Oppressed* (1970) he uses literacy, learning to read and write, which
seems to be a uniquely individual and personal agenda, as a tool for
exploring and promoting social change. He refers to this as
conscientization, awareness of self in context, a concept that simultaneously promotes personal and social transformation.

Here I believe is a fundamental paradox in the pursuit of peace.
Peacemaking embraces the challenge of personal transformation,

of pursuing awareness, growth, and commitment to change at a personal level. In protracted, violent conflicts, this transformation involves grief and trauma work, as well as dealing with deep feelings of fear, anger, and bitterness that accompany accumulated personal and family loss. Peacemaking equally involves the task and priority of systemic transformation, of increasing justice and equality in our world. It is the construction of global community involving the tasks of changing oppressive systems, sharing resources fairly, and promoting nonviolent resolution of conflict between peoples.

In sum, the Freire folly suggests that transformative peacemaking upholds and pursues both personal and systemic change.

Micah's Dilemma: The Paradox of Justice and Mercy

Wow!

The prophet Micah wrote that the task before us is to do justice, love mercy, and walk humbly with our God. From the perspective of peacemaking, the first two concepts pose an interesting paradox.

Doing justice is the pursuit of restoration, of rectifying wrongs, of creating right relationships based on equity and fairness. Pursuing justice involves advocacy for those harmed, for open acknowledgement of the wrongs committed, and for making things right.

Mercy, on the other hand, involves compassion, forgiveness, and a new start. Mercy is oriented toward supporting persons who have committed injustices, encouraging them to change and move on.

In peacemaking, we can feel the tension of these two necessary energies. Too often at times of intense conflict and division these two are posed as incompatible opposites. We either do justice or we forgive and forget. The unique challenge of the Micah dilemma is to uphold both: to pursue justice in ways that respect people and to achieve restoration of relationships based on recognizing and amending injustices. In fact we might suggest that reconciliation is best understood as the bringing together of justice and mercy in the context of fractured relationships. It assumes the proactive engagement of people in restoring what has been lost and starting anew. This paradox points us in the direction of a restorative process characterized by a passion for standing with the oppressed, embracing Truth, and making things right and a

Amen!

compassion for others, respecting even our enemies and reconciling relationships through understanding and forgiveness.

In other words, transformative peacemaking embraces both justice and mercy.

The Power Paradox: Empowerment and Interdependence

When we first initiated a year-long seminar in a number of squatter villages in Costa Rica, we struggled with the title we would give to the course. We ended up with *Capacitación Social* (Kavanaugh 1989). *Capacitación* is often translated as training. But that hardly captures its deeper image and meaning. The word is built on the root *capaz*, to be capable or able, which is synonymous with the Spanish verb *poder*. *Puedo* and *soy capaz*, are two ways of saying, "I can." However, *poder* is also the word for power. Thus, a better translation for our seminar title is "Social Empowerment." The notion of *capacitación* suggests a fundamental idea: Empowerment is overcoming the obstacles and making possible the movement from "I cannot" to "I can."

On the other hand, as the course evolved through meetings twice a week for more than a year, the single most discussed topic was how to create and nurture *confianza*, or trust. Empowerment of self was intimately wrapped up with empowerment of others through creating community. The notion of *confianza* suggested another key idea: Empowerment involves mutual dependence. "I can" is only fully accomplished with "I need you."

Peacemaking values both these elements. It works for the empowerment of people to be active and full participants in the decisions and environment that affect their lives. It understands empowerment as emerging in interdependent relationships and contributing back to the growth of others in community. Transformative peacemaking, then, empowers individuals and nurtures mutuality and community.

The Gandhi Dilemma: The Paradox of Process and Outcome

Ron Kraybill, a colleague from Mennonite Conciliation Service, coined a phrase we often use in our mediation work. "Process," he wrote, "matters more than outcome" (Kraybill, Lederach, and Price 1989). The logic of this idea is simply that at times of heated conflict too little attention is paid to how the issues are to be approached, discussed, and decided. There is a push toward solution and outcome that skips the discipline of creating an adequate and clear process for achieving an acceptable result. Process, it is argued, is the key to the Kingdom.

On the other hand, critics of mediation have argued that the field has become mesmerized, ad nauseam, with the techniques of process. Such mesmerism creates a blindspot to the broader issues of substance, especially when there are concerns of injustice and power imbalances, issues that become clear only as one focuses on the outcome (Merry and Milner 1993). Process as technique, it is argued, is a blind alley that only detracts from the real issue.

Mohandas Gandhi posed these two, process and outcome, as a paradox. Such an approach includes but moves beyond process as technique to understanding process as a philosophy and lifestyle; includes but moves beyond outcome as a result that gauges justice to understanding outcome as a commitment to Truth and restoration. On the one hand, the Gandhi dilemma invites us to embrace process as way of life that takes seriously the means by which we pursue our goals. It is undergirded by the values of participation, cooperation, and respect for others, even our enemies. On the other hand, it invites us to an ongoing commitment to Truth and restoration of relationships as the ultimate measure of sustainable outcome.

To reiterate, transformative peacemaking is based on understanding fair, respectful, and inclusive process as a way of life and envisions outcome as a commitment to increasing justice, seeking truth, and healing relationships.

Conclusion

In this chapter, I have outlined a number of elements that form the foundation of a framework for conflict transformation and building peace. Such a framework points to the key goals and values that guide the pedagogical project in peacemaking and can be summarized in the following goals:

1. Maintaining a broad conception of conflict and peace building that legitimates and encourages multiple roles relevant to different tasks in the progression of conflict.

2. Promoting the ultimate goals of increasing justice, reducing violence, and restoring broken relationships.

3. Developing opportunities for transformation, both personal and systemic.

4. Promoting a holistic view of conflict transformation as restoration that embraces justice, forgiveness, and reconciliation.

5. Pursuing social empowerment as the nurturing of individuals and community.

6. Understanding process as a way of life rather than as a technique and outcome as a commitment to Truth and sustained restoration rather than as agreements or results.

We can now return to the question of how this broader framework of building peace relates to training in conflict transformation across cultures. The framework suggests that such training is not merely an expansion of the field or the transfer of techniques, but rather the endeavor to pursue personal and systemic transformation and change. It further builds on the principle that our interaction and relationships must be based on mutual respect and that our training methods must blend with the ultimate outcomes we pursue. Thus, related to the objectives of this book, the framework raises the question of how one can approach the task of education and the development of appropriate conflict resolution mechanisms across and in diverse cultural settings. It further underscores the concern of integrity, of how to weave and blend the methodology with the ultimate values and goals espoused in the field, with special attention to how such a blend is achieved as we cross cultural boundaries.

or here.

3

An Integrated Framework for Training

The reflections, ideas, and suggestions I will put forward about conflict resolution training did not emerge in a vacuum. The evolution of my approach to training and the analytical models I will describe are indebted to at least three major schools of thought and action: popular education, particularly of the Freirean school; appropriate technology emerging from the field of international development; and ethnographic research. I have found them to be useful and thought-provoking parallels, although they are rarely related directly to the field of conflict resolution. Each of the schools has contributed to my work as a trainer, researcher, and practitioner. I believe the ideas in each area are philosophical if not spiritual cousins of the peacemaking framework and lie at the heart of the training-project agenda. In this chapter, I will provide a brief description of how I understand both their concern with and contribution to our endeavor.

Popular Education

The work of Paulo Freire and my own direct contact with many efforts at popular education in Latin America and Africa are perhaps the most important influences on my thinking and training activity.[1] The popular education movement is so rich and diverse as to make it difficult to attempt a summary that does it justice. However, the following points from the writings of Freire and the subsequent movement in popular education have impressed me:

First, education is never neutral. It always involves a project ultimately aimed either at keeping things as they are or changing them. Popular education promotes change both in social and educational systems. It is centered on the concept of conscientization, the process of building awareness of self-in-context that produces individual growth and social change.

Second, popular education is a process of mutuality. Student and teacher discover and learn together through reflection and action, which are kept in direct relationship as the root of learning and transformation.

Third, people and their everyday understandings are key resources. Their knowledge and experiences are a vast and usually untapped library to be probed and excited. Their knowledge must be validated and trusted. This suggests a fundamental principle: from the perspective of training, people are resources not recipients.

Finally, posing problems relative to real-life situations and challenges rather than providing prescriptions about those situations is an important pedagogical tool. It stimulates reflection and simultaneously encourages people to trust their ability yet transcend themselves and participate actively in identifying the challenges they face and the means to meet them. It gives them the power of naming the world, their experience, and their journey.

What I have found particularly challenging about the perspective of popular education is its critical attention not only to the proposed goals or content of pedagogical projects, but also to the role of process as the carrier of both culture and ideology. This perspective entails a particularly strong critique of the premise underlying formal Western education as based on prescriptive

1. Key references in popular education include Freire 1970, Hope and Timmel 1988, and Marins et al. 1988. For a good description and outline of popular education related to conflict transformation, see Chupp 1991.

mechanisms for learning. Prescription, Freire writes, is a key element in the relationship between oppressor and oppressed. "To exist, humanly, is to *name* the world, to change it. Once named, the world in its turn reappears to the namers as a problem and requires of them a new *naming*" (Freire 1970, 76). This act of naming is the right of every person, Freire argues, so that no one can name the world for another in a "prescriptive act which robs others of their words." He, of course, is not engaged here in literal semantics. He is fundamentally concerned about education as process. Thus, the key issue pushed from the perspective of popular education is how to create a process that is consistent with the outcome goals of empowerment and transformation that the educational project purports to achieve.

It is, of course, important to keep this approach in context. Popular education can be misunderstood and abused, particularly where it creates a de facto glorification of indigenous knowledge as a panacea. The same can be said if this misunderstanding translates into a refusal to actively participate as a facilitator or trainer with one's own experience or knowledge on the premise that it may disrupt the purity of native processes. The fundamental idea of popular education is not to keep people in the dark or demand of them what cannot be delivered. It is oriented at building an education process that is appropriate to the context and that validates the knowledge and resources people have available in that context, as opposed to building an educational process that circumvents their context and experience.

Appropriate Technology

From education we switch now to the cutting edge of development theory and practice, appropriate technology—what insiders often call A.T. My contact with A.T. has come primarily through visits, conversations, and work with a colleague in Guatemala, Jacob Schiere. Jacob directed an appropriate technology center and worked with indigenous community "promoters" throughout Guatemala. They were perhaps best known for their work in dry latrines, alternative stoves, and efforts at indigenous medicine and health. I had the opportunity of associating with some of them briefly on the challenge of conflict as it related to their presence in rural areas of Guatemala, an undertaking that placed them at the heart of the violent swirl engulfing the country's political and social landscape. Schiere and I talked about many things, but what stands out in my mind are three elements that consistently were at the core of how appropriate technology conceptualizes its purpose and work (Schiere 1991).

First, appropriate technology is founded on the critique that transfer-based development is problematic. This critique suggests that although technology, especially in its mechanized forms, represents concrete and measurable things, its transfer from one setting to another neither assures nor even at times promotes development. This is particularly true because so much of technology and development is seen in Western terms of solving problems by introducing gadgets. That is, problems are solved and progress is made through mechanical devices. Thus, the transfer mentality of taking what works in modernized, dominant settings to traditional ones often produces the inverse effect of what was desired. The gadgets of development from one setting sit rusted and wasted in another. Or in a worst-case scenario, the technology replaces indigenous approaches with imported methods that are hard to sustain and simultaneously may eliminate long-standing traditions and resources.

The A.T. critique raises the concern for sustainable development and led to the approach that the problem-solving must be understood in a broader context. Recent authors, such as Seidman and Frederick (1992), suggest that development is not just the task of responding to immediate problems, but rather the challenge of sustaining change. Fundamentally, this kind of approach indicates that the technology best suited for a particular problem and setting— be it in the field of agriculture, health, or housing—must be rooted and applicable in that setting. Thus, the starting point for appropriate technology is seeking solutions in the setting not outside it.

Second, appropriate technology focuses on discovering resources that are available and local. The idea is not simply that you teach people to fish rather than give them food; more importantly, they fish in their own ponds! This approach means that our search for resources broadens beyond the material and mechanical. Providing solutions to problems does not exclusively involve inventing a new gadget. It must include what we have available at hand, what we know about it, and the way we think about and use what is available.

Third, appropriate technology places primary emphasis on tapping indigenous knowledge about the problem at hand. Paul Richards (1985), speaking in reference to his experiences and research in West Africa, went as far as writing that "indigenous agricultural knowledge" is the single most immobilized resource in agricultural development in that setting.

In sum, appropriate technology thinking has several ramifications. First, it suggests that indigenous knowledge, and by indigenous I refer to people from a given setting, is a resource that must be pursued, encouraged, and validated. Second, it suggests that the knowledge of a person in the setting becomes a useful tool when it interacts with others from the setting, with a focus on the realities and problems they face. Thus, sharing with each other what we face and what we know is a resource for resolving problems and creating community ultimately related to sustainable solutions in our setting.

Ethnography

From education and development, our attention turns to social science research and to the methodology of ethnography. Ethnography is best known as a research method in anthropology and sociology (Spradley 1979). In their classical form, ethnographies were the detailed descriptions and studies anthropologists made of remote villages, people, and their way of living and doing. In contemporary research, ethnography combined with participant observation has emerged as an important method for studying modern-day phenomena and social settings from hospitals and jails to social movements and political campaigns. Most relevant to our discussion here are the principles and philosophy that underlie the ethnographic approach and mindset in social science research.

Ethnography starts from the premise that little is known and much must be discovered about a particular social phenomenon or setting. Its goal is the discovery and description of relevant and meaningful categories of action as created and understood by the very persons producing the action. This goal is accomplished through intensive study of people in their natural setting, where, so to speak, "the action is." Ethnographers sometimes borrow a term from archeology and refer to this as "in situ" research. (In archeology this means that the records produced of finds are studied in their original found position.) Social science research in situ refers to a kind of archeology of social knowledge that involves sifting through the layers of accumulated natural knowledge necessary for creating meaningful human action, encounters, and social structures in any given setting.

Ethnographers try to make sense of action and meaning by understanding it through the eyes and experiences of those creating it. This is referred to as an emic approach, where the meaning and categories for understanding are taken not from the researcher but rather from the members under study (Geertz 1981). Primary emphasis is placed on describing what people do and how they interpret their behavior and action: that is, how the people themselves make sense of the things they do. Thus, direct observation of what people do in their natural setting and their taken-for-granted knowledge—discovered through their talk in and about their setting and action—are the most important and useful resources for uncovering the relevant categories.

To conclude, the mindset of ethnography suggests two relevant ideas. First, it inculcates an enormous respect for how people in a given setting understand themselves and events happening in that setting. Second, it pays careful attention to everyday talk and taken-for-granted meaning in that setting. From a research perspective, key discoveries about categories of action and meaning emerge from the most common of expressions and knowledge.

Conclusion

We can now identify some of the key concerns emerging from these three perspectives and suggest an integrated framework useful for our analysis and critique of conflict resolution training. I have graphically summarized those in figure 3, a summary that includes these central ideas.

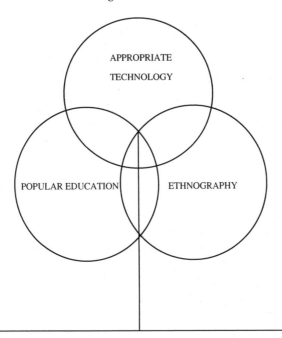

1. People in setting are a key resource, not recipients.

2. Indigenous knowledge is a pipeline to discovery, meaning, and appropriate action.

3. Participation of local people in the process is central.

4. Building from available local resources fosters self-sufficiency and sustainability.

5. Empowerment involves a process that fosters awareness-of-self in context and validates discovery, naming, and creation through reflection and action.

Figure 3
The Heart of the Matter: An Integrated Framework
for Empowerment

We begin with the fundamental view that people in a given setting are a key resource in the educational process. Their understanding of that setting and of themselves comprises the pipeline to discovery of important categories of thought, meaning-in-context, and creative action. Related to conflict transformation more specifically, this integrated framework suggests that identifying, understanding, and handling problems in a setting is best accomplished through participation and empowerment of people within that setting. In the long run, building on local and available resources fosters self-sufficiency and helps sustain development and change over time.

Further, the integrated framework suggests that empowerment emerges from processes that permit and promote self-awareness and validate direct participation in discovering, naming, and creating appropriate responses to identified needs and problems. This is a holistic understanding of growth and learning that emerges through a continuous cycle of reflection-action-reflection. The integration of these elements can be understood as social empowerment in line with the peacemaking framework suggested in the preceding chapter.

Athough this integrated framework provides a broader basis for understanding training in general, we can initially explore a number of specific commonalities and critiques that emerge as we connect these approaches with the field of conflict transformation training. The foundation and practice of conflict transformation share much of what has just been described. Mediation, for example, places a high value on participation, on people's identifying and working out solutions to their own problems, and on building self-awareness and contributing to positive social change. However, as noted earlier, the integrated framework would suggest that these values are relevant and applicable not only to the practice of mediation, but also to the methodology of training and to the creation of mediation models and approaches. This book is aimed at raising issue with how we approach the pedagogical project, that is with the method of training.

It is my contention that mainstream training in the field of mediation in North America has followed, in broad strokes, a form of education based more on prescription and the transfer of knowledge than on conscientization and participation as described here. In my experience, the prescriptive nature of our methodology makes little if any adjustment as we move across cultural and class lines. Metaphorically, we tend to translate our materials into another language, rather than create them in situ. The integrated framework, I believe, provides a theoretical base that raises important questions about how our methodology blends with our ultimate-outcome goals and values, particularly as related to training in nondominant cultural settings. In the following chapters, I wish to push out this proposition more fully through the development of two comparative training approaches and their characteristics.

PART TWO

Rethinking Approaches to Training

4

An Analytical Approach to Training

In 1984, I had the opportunity to prepare a series of workshops on conflict resolution and mediation for groups of church leaders in Central America. For some time, I had been interested in the question of culture and conflict. Having lived in Spanish-speaking settings, I was convinced there were important differences in how people from diverse cultural backgrounds handled conflict. As I prepared for these workshops I worked hard not to lay a North American model of conflict resolution on the participants. I went to the literature, but found precious little in the field. I read novels and social scientists from Latin America, culling out ideas and some case studies. I interviewed quite a number of people from Central America about their family and community conflicts and problems. In the end, I prepared a brief manual and workshop to be delivered in Spanish (Lederach 1986).

The training began in Guatemala. The four-day event seemed to go well overall, but one incident stands out very clearly in my mind. We had reached the mediation aspect of the training. In preparation for this component I had put together some fifteen role plays, all of them developed from real-life situations in Central America. As I had always done, and as I had always seen other mediation trainers do, I started the introduction to mediation by providing an overview of the process and then giving a direct demonstration through a role play. The situation was a family conflict and I invited two participants from the group to take the roles of a father and an adult daughter, and I took the part of the mediator. I had developed the role play directly from a situation that had been described to me by a Guatemalan. The demonstration took about an hour, and in the end we reached some understanding between the two.

I then opened the floor for observations, comments, and questions. The first person to speak did not address himself to me, but rather to his two compatriots, and said a single sentence, "You two looked liked *gringos*!" That comment has stuck with me ever since. It was an eye-opener and represented what I sometimes humorously refer to as my "Kuhnian paradigmatic shift." The materials were in Spanish. The role play was from Guatemala. We did it in fluent Spanish. The two disputants were Guatemalan. "What was there in this process," I kept asking myself, "that could take two Guatemalans and turn them into *gringos*?"

I have arrived at the conclusion that there were at least two key elements, each of which I will explore in more detail in later chapters. First, embedded implicitly in the mediation process I presented were fundamental assumptions about conflict and how to handle it that were appropriate and applicable in one cultural setting but not necessarily shared by another. This insight led to an important shift in my research questions (Lederach 1985). Prior to this, I had gone along with most practitioners in the field in asking: What cultural differences and nuances exist among Central Americans that need to be taken into account as we work at conflict resolution? My question now turned in the opposite direction: What are the cultural assumptions of the North American model of mediation?

Second, and perhaps more important, embedded subtly in my training project was the unintended residue of imperialism. Difficult to admit, and even more difficult to recognize, the outcome was clear for those who had eyes to see. The cultural assumptions of my context were moved to theirs with the underlying premise that mine were the right way to go and that they should learn them. I have struggled since, within myself and alongside other

colleagues, with the disconcerting question of whether our training process in conflict resolution is disconnected from the ultimate
goals we espouse. This shift raised key questions for me that are
at the heart of this book and that have been at the root of my slow
and long experiment with cross-cultural training. My prevailing
question is no longer: How do we adapt our conflict resolution
model to a Hispanic context? Too often, I have discovered I am
really asking: How do we fit Hispanics into our model? Rather
my concern is this: How do we foster a pedagogical project that
respects and empowers people to understand, participate in creating, and strengthen appropriate models for working at conflict
in their own context?

The Basis of Training

In the ensuing chapters I want to get at this question by comparing two approaches to training. I have arrived at these approaches through the slow and sometimes grinding gristmill of
experience more than by way of pure theoretical endeavor. I say
slow and grinding to emphasize my own mistakes past and
present and to reemphasize that my ideas and suggestions are in
constant evolution and experimentation. They should not be taken
as final conclusions or set in concrete; but are approximations
aimed at answering some of the toughest questions facing the field
of conflict transformation as it gains momentum and finds itself
moving across and working between cultures.

The two approaches to training, which I will refer to as the
prescriptive and the *elicitive*, should be understood as analytic models, or as Weber would call them, "ideal types" (Weber 1947). In
other words, in real life the exact, pure model of either type may
not exist. I am creating a description of each in order to compare
and contrast. These models will permit us to envision a spectrum
of possibilities.

In the following pages, I will present two models as representing extreme ends of a spectrum, each with a defining set of characteristics. I will use them for comparative purposes, and I do not
assume that they exactly match how training happens in real life.
Educators and trainers in nonviolence, mediation, and conflict

transformation may find that their work has aspects of both models. My own style in fact varies from setting to setting and from training to training, and has aspects of both. I am using the models and their corresponding characteristics to permit an exploration of key concerns, to offer a constructive critique of our approach to training, and to point a direction for positive change in the ways we approach and understand the relationship between conflict, culture, and training.

It should be clearly stated, however, that in using a comparative polemic, I am not suggesting one model is right or superior to another. Both have strengths and weaknesses, and combinations of them are likely to hold the most potential. What I am after in the development of the ideal types is the necessary and initial task of establishing a paradigm useful for analysis and, then at a later stage, the projection of application in real-life settings.

In the following chapters, I will concentrate on describing major characteristics and differences between the prescriptive and elicitive approaches. Prior to exploring differences, it is crucial to recognize the fundamental basis of any training or educational project and the commonalities these models share. I believe this foundation and commonality is social knowledge.

Social Knowledge: The Basis of Conflict and Training

As a starting point, I would suggest that training of any nature is based on either the creation or the dissemination of social knowledge, perhaps on both. Closer to our concerns, training in conflict transformation is based on social knowledge about conflict, how it operates, and how to handle it. By its very nature, conflict is a phenomenon that everyone has experienced. All of us have developed what can be referred to as a bank of social knowledge about conflict. Correspondingly, an analytical approach to training about conflict will legitimately involve the development of a conceptual framework for comparing how various training methods understand and use this bank. I think this is best done by returning to several of the key assumptions of a constructionist approach regarding conflict and considering those in the context of how social knowledge and meaning are achieved.

Earlier I asserted that conflict is socially constructed. By this I mean that conflict does not just happen, it is created. Key in this creation process are social knowledge, the meaning that people attach to events and issues, and what, correspondingly, is appropriate response and action to take. A framework for understanding what comprises this conflict knowledge and how it is used has at least three aspects—expression, perception, and interpretation—that are perhaps best described through communication theory (Watzlawick et al. 1978).

In figure 4, I have outlined the steps of a simple communication sequence between two people, based on the popular saying, "I see what you mean." The outline suggests two major divisions: first, between the two people and second, between what is internal to the person, and thereby unavailable and nonpalpable to the outside world, and what is available and observable in the social world. Within the sequence, we then have three key schemes, each based on knowledge and meaning.[1]

The sequence begins with what I call here the expressive scheme, representing a mechanism or a vehicle by which intended meaning is expressed. It is through this scheme that our ideas and intent enter the world. Underpinning this mechanism, however, is the knowledge base about how expression of intent is to be accomplished. In terms of conflict, expressive schemes may take the form of everything from silence, to eye movement, to verbal persuasion or physical assault. This scheme, for example, raises the question of what mechanism is most appropriate to register my dissension when I find myself at odds with someone's behavior. Key to this first step is the accumulated, often taken-for-granted, social and cultural knowledge about how, in what circumstances, and by what means the intended meaning is conveyed. Through this expressive scheme, communicative movement is made from "What I mean" to "See what I mean." Through this vehicle, something is created that is visible and palpable in the social world.

1. P. H. Gullivers in his important text on cross-cultural conflict, *Disputes and Negotiations*, develops what he refers to as a "cyclical" model of negotiation that has key parallels to the communication base developed in Figure 4.

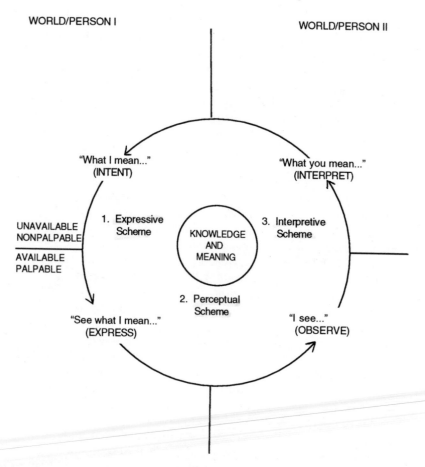

Figure 4
Communication and Conflict Schemes

The second step moves to the perceptual scheme. Perception involves the question of what we are attentive to in the world. In other words, the perceptual mechanism is built on social knowledge related to what our senses are accustomed to and trained to watch for, listen to, or intuit. In terms of conflict, this scheme raises the question of what we pay attention to that provide signs of something being not right in the relationship. In Central America, for example, a slight movement of the eyes may indicate embarrassment, showing respect, or disagreement. The perceptive scheme involves whether we are paying attention to those movements to observe signs of the intended meaning. Perception is the "I see" portion of the everyday phrase.

The third step involves interpretation. The interpretive scheme is a mechanism by which meaning is given to what is observed. And here we need to draw on the theoretical proposals of how meaning is constructed, which are clearly delineated in the works of Schutz (1967), Blumer (1969), and Berger and Luckman (1967). According to these theoreticians, meaning emerges through an act of comparison. Something has meaning when it is compared and contrasted with other things—a process accomplished by locating any given object, event, or word in our bank of knowledge. Interpretation thus involves a process of making sense of something by placing it in relationship with other things that are already known.

Returning to eye movement as an example, in an Asian setting, looking down is interpreted as a sign of respect. In a North American setting, however, we may be told to "Look at me when I am talking to you," indicating that downcast eyes are a sign of disrespect or of not paying attention. Depending on where and with what we locate or relate downcast eyes, an entirely different meaning emerges. This is the basic mechanism by which reframing functions (Watzlawick et al. 1978). Reframing is the process of relocating something in a different place and relating it to different things so as to give a different meaning.

Let me give another illustration. When my son was younger he resisted going to a babysitter. For him, babysitting meant being left behind without mom and dad. This became a more significant problem when both of us worked and needed to leave him for longer periods. We solved the problem when we discovered that he viewed his older sister's "going to school" as something desirable. As long as we referred to his morning caretaker as a teacher and to his experience as school, he went enthusiastically. If we slipped and referred to it as babysitting, he reacted and resisted. Here was a simple example of the reframing process wherein different meanings can be attached to the same objective set of facts or events. What creates meaning is precisely the act of locating a given thing in relationship to other things providing a new frame of reference. This is the interpretive process.

The interpretive scheme places what has been observed in a context that gives it meaning. This scheme completes the movement from "I see" to "What you mean." However, we are only able to locate something in our own accumulated bank of knowledge. Thus, as was explained in the above examples, what I see is given meaning by how I locate it in my knowledge, but it may or may not correspond to the original intention that was conveyed by the other.

The overall sequence in figure 4 raises some useful questions about culture and conflict at several levels. On the practitioner side, we recognize that each of the schemes is accomplished on the basis of accumulated social knowledge relevant to a person's experience and cultural background, underscoring the complexity of cross-cultural communication and construction of shared social meaning, particularly at times of conflict. But more important from the perspective of this book are the key questions of whose social conflict knowledge is relevant for developing appropriate models and how such knowledge can become an explicit training resource. In this regard, we can identify an important analytical distinction between an implicit and an explicit knowledge base, and how it is used and understood in conflict resolution training.

Implicit social conflict knowledge refers to everyday understandings accumulated through natural experience. Life's experiences provide us with commonsense knowledge about how conflict operates generally. More specifically, we also have accumulated an understanding of how conflict operates in our given milieu of origin and how it is handled in our cultural context. However, this knowledge base is taken-for-granted and often is not seen as anything more than what everybody knows.

On the other hand, contrasted with everyday understanding is *explicit* experience and knowledge. I am referring to a focused, intentional effort to increase one's knowledge about conflict and how to handle it. Through study, reading, research, training, and

IMPLICIT CONFLICT KNOWLEDGE

1. Common sense understanding
   of social conflict

2. Everyday experience in real-life conflicts

3. Natural experience with conflicts
   in cultural setting

4. Natural conflict management
   practices in setting

EXPLICIT CONFLICT KNOWLEDGE

1. Knowledge about conflict
   through study

2. Focused experience on
   conflict resolution practices

3. Specialization in one or
   several settings/areas

4. Conflict resolution model
   dissemination

Figure 5

Knowledge as the Basis of Training

focused experience people build knowledge relevant to conflict. I will refer to this knowledge as expertise, making note that specialization and professionalization often follow this knowledge base. Thus, people accumulating explicit conflict knowledge and experience are considered experts and, correspondingly, are those who train others. This analytical distinction between knowledge bases establishes two types of participants in a training event: those who train and those who are trained.

Figure 5 summarizes the characteristics of each group of participants. What is vital from an analytical perspective is how these knowledge bases are treated socially. Implicit knowledge is rarely sought after, nor understood as a resource, yet explicit conflict knowledge is socially valued as a commodity. It is in fact explicit knowledge that can be packaged and given a monetary value. This point is crucial in developing an analytical framework for conflict resolution training, for it establishes two key propositions.

First, it suggests that both knowledge bases are present in any given training. Second, it postulates that the relevance, importance, and role of the two knowledge bases will vary according to the training model. These propositions are the basis for exploring and distinguishing between the prescriptive and elicitive training models described in the next chapters.

Conclusion

In this chapter, we have established an analytical framework for looking at conflict resolution training. The framework is built on social conflict knowledge as the key to both the development of conflict intervention models and the basis of training. We suggested that the fundamental mechanisms by which conflict is constructed and handled, and on which training is based, are rooted in schemes of action and interpretation emerging from accumulated social and cultural knowledge. Analytically, we further distinguished between two knowledge bases creating two distinct participant groups in training. On the one hand, we identified the trainee community, which is assumed to have a base of implicit, everyday knowledge about conflict. On the other is the trainer or expert community, whose role emerges on the explicit, or specialized, conflict knowledge and experience accumulated above and beyond the implicit base. From an analytical perspective, how these two knowledge bases are socially valued and treated is a key question in differentiating approaches to conflict resolution training.

This brief overview of social knowledge as the basis of training provides us with a series of perspectives that the prescriptive and elicitive models will now attempt to flesh out. In the following chapters, I will address analytically several key questions related to the variation of how social conflict knowledge is seen and valued. These questions include: Whose knowledge forms the foundation of the training, and how is each valued? What are the roles that trainers and participants take in the training event? What are the assumptions and goals of the training? What are the methods by which these goals are pursued? We will tackle these questions by descriptively outlining the prescriptive and elicitive models of training.

5

The Prescriptive Model

How to prevent and resolve public controversy." "A how-to-do-it package." "Develop new skills." "Make conflict work for you." "Enhance your ability to deal with difficult people." "Develop the necessary skills to respond constructively to conflict." The lines leap out from a stack of conflict resolution and mediation brochures that cross my desk. The promises of training often point to what I consider the unspoken motto of the prescriptive model: "We have just what you need."

Sifting through training announcements and brochures, I am simultaneously struck with the powerful vision of practical peacemaking and the realization that conflict resolution and mediation are seeking a professional niche in North American society. For many people, one of the key mechanisms providing financial stability to this new field is the area of training—of packaging and selling the knowledge. Thus, most trainings are conceived to deliver a product. A certain pattern of questions and promises about training emerge in the training brochures: What is it? What will the training include? Who needs it? Why is it important? The description outlines the delivery of strategies, techniques, skills, models, and methods for meeting this defined need. Training is seen as an event and a package of how to's.

My purpose in this chapter is to construct and outline in broad strokes the key characteristics of a "pure" prescriptive approach to training. By pure I mean to reduce the model to its bare essentials in order to create an ideal type for the purpose of comparative analysis. For the moment, we will bracket the question of culture and will assume that the training event takes place in a setting where participants and trainers share a common culture and language. Constructing such a model involves describing various aspects of the training, with an eye toward making more explicit the assumptions that underlie the approach. The pure side of the description suggests we will exaggerate certain aspects and leave out others in order to highlight the extreme case. An economist, for example, might describe the characteristics of a capitalist as a type of economic behavior. That description will attempt to outline key aspects but will not correspond exactly to any given person. Such is our endeavor here. I wish to outline and make explicit the key aspects and characteristics of a prescriptive approach to conflict resolution training that may not correspond exactly to any given training event.

The Training Event: Roles and Elements

As a starting point, we can describe the trainer. Essentially, the prescriptive model understands the trainer as an expert. The training event is built around his or her specialized knowledge and experience in conflict resolution. That expertise is often brought together in the form of a model presented to participants. The model is made up of strategies suggesting how conflict is resolved and presents techniques to implement the strategic approach. Learning and mastering the model is the primary goal of the event. I have graphically attempted to lay out the overview of this model in figure 6. Several key assumptions underlie this approach.

First, the prescriptive approach, in its pure form, assumes that the expert knows what the participants need. In other words, primary control and design of the training lies with the trainer. In many cases, particularly in our market economy, the expert may bring together several packages, and participants self-select the one filling their need. This is what we might refer to as a menu

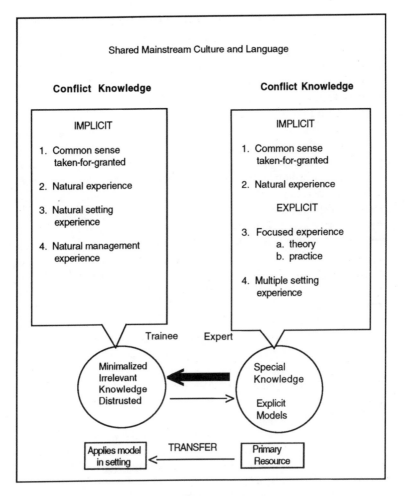

Figure 6
Prescription/Expertise: The Transfer Model

approach to training. For example, in mediation, people begin with the introductory level, but may go on to receive specialized training in divorce, public policy, or organizational arenas. Nonetheless, the training event is conducted by a predefined agenda designed to meet predefined need. The definitions of both the need and agenda tend to lie primarily in the realm of and are based on the trainer's expertise.

Second, throughout the event, the explicit and expert knowledge of the trainer is assumed to be and is valued as more trustworthy and relevant than that of the participants. Correspondingly, the participants' knowledge is assumed, by and large, to be less relevant and credible in the context and content of the training. The experts' knowledge is central and the participants' knowledge is peripheral.

Third, the primary goal of the training is to learn the model. This is accomplished through a transfer dynamic and structure where participants try to take on the knowledge and skills necessary to implement the model. Through a prescriptive mode, the trainer provides a series of exercises and presentations aimed at teaching participants how to understand and carry out the approach. Implicitly, to do the approach well, participants emulate and try to work like the expert. In other words, transferability is valued positively, assumed to be beneficial, and pursued as a desired end.

These assumptions and elements are replicated in the methods followed in the training process. Consider the following chronological description of a typical introductory mediation training event.

1. The training begins with a cognitive description of the model presented through readings, lectures, and visual graphics. "This is *what* we do."

2. The cognitive description is followed by exemplary demonstrations led by the trainer. Through visual and participatory demonstration the trainer fleshes out the strategy and technique. "This is *how* we do it."

3. Participants practice and interact with the approach, or parts of it, through role plays and other exercises. In most instances, these exercises are developed ahead of time for the purpose of practicing various aspects of the model. "Here, try the model out for yourself in this situation."

4. Feedback and evaluation is provided from the trainer. The feedback reiterates the model. "This is the model. This is where you went awry. This is what I might have tried."

5. The training includes the opportunity for questions and answers. Participants raise questions of "what if?" Trainers provide responses of "here's how."

In the pure-type approach, application and practice are highly valued. Participants are afforded ample opportunity to experiment with, learn, and take on the approaches and techniques prescribed. This approach is understood and presented as skill building. Emphasis is placed on the techniques, both conceptual and strategic, underlying the model. This induction in the approach, techniques, and skills is seen as an introductory first step toward practice in real cases. In most instances, those with interest and who show promise continue the training process by working with more experienced practitioners in live situations.

The Training Approach

What we see in the prescriptive model, both at the conceptual level and reinforced through the actual method of teaching, is the primary role of the trainer's knowledge as the key resource to be transferred to and emulated by the participants. There is a heavy flow from trainer to participant and a light flow back in terms of model creation and application. The training event focuses on trainees mastering the model through cognitive understanding of the strategies and practical experimentation with the techniques and skills.

In this pure-type approach, the cultural and ideological underpinnings of the model are rarely made explicit; they are, however, the very elements that tend to emerge from the context where the model was developed. Within a prescriptive modality, culture is often seen as an additional level of sophistication and expertise added to the repertoire of the already trained. Thus, culture is not seen as embedded in the model presented. Rather, the conflict resolution model and its modalities and techniques are culturally neutral. In this approach to training, we find a synthesis of two important orientations: the desirability of technical transfer and a high view of the universality of the technology.

The purpose and usefulness of the prescriptive approach lie in its capacity to outline and permit participants to interact with an approach to conflict resolution and to understand and master the particular strategies and techniques it entails. For many people seeking to expand their understanding of how conflict works and how to better handle it, the models represent concrete ideas and approaches. There is opportunity provided for new thinking, improving skills, and feeling more confident about what to do when faced with conflict, all of which is experienced as empowering.

On the other side, the transfer-based training method establishes at an implicit level several key elements as regards both the content and the relationship between trainer and trainee. The trainer defines the need, names the model, provides the content based on special knowledge, oversees the process, and provides direction and correction. The goal of learning for participants is to understand and master the model. Further, the transfer methodology is accomplished more readily through teachable units. Thus, the prescriptive modality tends to reduce conflict resolution to technology—to technique and skill, which become key aspects both of the training and of the subsequent application of the model.

As we will discuss in more detail later, the prescriptive methodology mixes together several important features of the content and model. Prescription rarely distinguishes between underlying broader social functions of conflict resolution and the more specific forms presented to fulfill those functions. It is important, however, to recognize that this distinction is central in working across cultures.

The social functions of conflict resolution refer to basic and more universal social processes and human needs. We could say that these basic functions may include elements such as those identified by Gulliver (1979)—for example, the need to understand and locate what a conflict is about, the need to create a proper forum or arena for addressing the concerns, or the need to be heard, to participate, and to have one's concerns taken seriously. The forms, however, would relate to the specific mechanisms or techniques developed to address these needs and processes.

Let me provide an example. We can say that in the midst of conflict people want to be heard and understood. A form for listening presented as a skill is paraphrasing. However, there are many other forms that might meet this basic need. Paraphrasing is an oral, verbal response mechanism. In some settings, as I have experienced with some Native Americans, silence shows respect and listening. In some Asian settings, you have to move beyond listening to attentive observation. If your primary focus is on the spoken vehicle, you may entirely miss the message.

In terms of our analysis, the prescriptive approach, by operating on a transfer modality, presents a conflict resolution model that assumes universality of both the basic social function and the more particular social form created to fulfill this need. This specific technique is thus presumed to be universal and in fact is the primary substance transferred through the training.

Conclusion

This bare-bones and rather coarse description of the prescriptive model may well seem exaggerated and unfair to trainers. Our purpose here was not to describe with exact precision any given training event, but rather to create the fundamental components of an analytically comparable model. We have done that by identifying a number of central characteristics of the model in its pure form.

The overview suggests the prescriptive approach is built on the premises of transferability and universality. Success is usually accomplished by presenting a specific model or approach that is understood by studying and learning to master the specific techniques presented. The methodology is one that presents the trainer as an expert in the model and the trainees as those seeking to take on the knowledge of the trainer and learn the model. The overall process is then understood as a training event, the format and agenda of which is proposed and defined primarily by the trainer to meet predefined needs. We now turn our attention to a similar description of the elicitive approach, prior to considering in more detail the strengths and weaknesses of each.

6

The Elicitive Model

We have no brochures announcing elicitive training, nor many real-life training events on which to base our analysis. Nonetheless, in the following pages, I wish to describe the distinguishing characteristics of a model of training that lies at the opposite end of the spectrum from the prescriptive approach. At this point, our purpose is to make explicit the key aspects of how the pure elicitive model approaches conflict resolution and mediation training. In subsequent chapters, I will outline a number of exercises and training formats that emerge from an elicitive frame of reference.

The elicitive approach starts from the vantage point that training is an opportunity aimed primarily at discovery, creation, and solidification of models that emerge from the resources present in a particular setting and respond to needs in that context. Its motto, borrowed from the theme of appropriate technology, suggests this concern: Discovering ways to catch fish in our own ponds. The emphasis is not only on empowerment as participating in creating models, but also in seeking resource and root in the cultural context itself.

For descriptive and analytical purposes, let us assume a trainer who comes from one cultural-linguistic context is working with participants who share a different language and cultural setting. As outlined in figure 7, our description of the elicitive approach will seek to answer relevant questions about the goals of the training, how trainers and participants understand their roles, and the fundamental elements involved in the training process.

The Training Roles

The starting point of elicitive training involves a reconceptualization of roles. On the one hand, the trainer sees himself or herself primarily as a catalyst and a facilitator rather than as an expert in a particular model of conflict resolution. Therefore, the key contribution of the trainer-as-catalyst does not lie primarily with the expertise the trainer may possess about the operation and skills inherent in a particular approach to conflict resolution or mediation. Rather it lies with the facilitating skill of providing opportunity for discovery and creation through an educative process that is highly participatory in nature.

Correspondingly, the participants and their knowledge are seen as the primary resource for the training, whether or not they initially see themselves as such. By knowledge-as-resource I refer to the often implicit but rich understandings people have about their setting. Included is their knowledge about how conflict emerges and develops among them and about how people try to handle and manage that conflict. Also included are their understandings about what things mean; that is, how language, perception, interpretation, and meaning are constructed around events and interactions in their context. Simply put, the foundation of this approach is that this implicit indigenous knowledge about ways of being and doing is a valued resource for creating and sustaining appropriate models of conflict resolution in a given setting.

Even in its purest form this approach does not exclude comparison with and study of other models. However, outside approaches are bracketed, that is, put off as secondary, in the early phases of the training. Primary emphasis is placed on first discovering and identifying what people already have in place and already know about the strengths and weaknesses of their own models of conflict resolution. Although the participants' knowledge is trusted, this trust is not directed at the glorification of in-

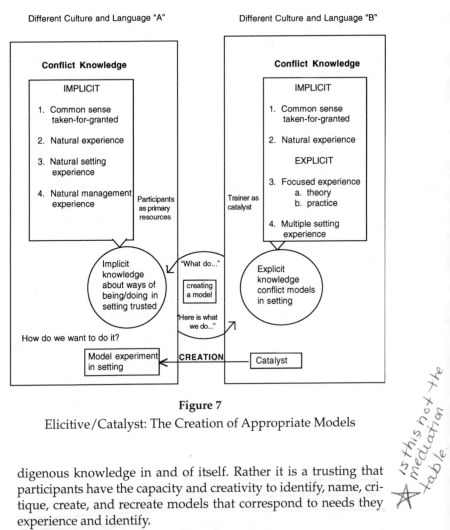

Figure 7

Elicitive/Catalyst: The Creation of Appropriate Models

digenous knowledge in and of itself. Rather it is a trusting that participants have the capacity and creativity to identify, name, critique, create, and recreate models that correspond to needs they experience and identify.

Starting from these premises, the trainer assumes a perspective of ignorance at two levels. First, at a very broad level, the design and goals of the training are identified and formulated by the participants rather than determined a priori by the trainer. Such a process can also take place in the prescriptive approach to the degree that people are seeking help because of a felt need.

Generally, the prescriptive model would suggest that a prepackaged training fits that need. Elicitive training begins with a more open approach of identifying the needs in a given context and then working with the participants to create the training that corresponds to the needs. Among other things, this approach leaves wide open the possibility that participants may wish to pursue areas of conflict transformation that have little to do with a given package. For example, participants may identify the need to work on nonviolent confrontation, or mediation, or trauma-healing work, or all three together.

A second aspect of "ignorance" relates to a more specific level of training. It suggests that the trainer not assume that his/her experience and expertise accumulated in one setting is the key resource for the training in another. Although the trainer may have many important and relevant experiences in a variety of settings, in the elicitive approach, these are not presented as the central core of the training process, but rather are bracketed in order to permit a participatory process of discovery. The attitude of the trainer is essentially, "I do not have the answer, but I can work together with others on a process that may help us find it."

The Training Approach

The elicitive nature of the training is accomplished through at least five interrelated kinds of activities. These can be arranged in chronological sequence; however, they also represent attitudes and goals throughout the training process. For descriptive purposes, I will outline them here as distinct, sequential elements in the training process as depicted in figure 8.

Discovery. The first set of activities are exercises aimed at participants engaging and interacting with their own understandings of how conflict and their response to it operate in their setting. These activities create a catalyst for people to think about implicit knowledge as a resource. To make commonsense knowledge a resource involves both discovery and description. The activities place before people questions such as: "What do we do?" and "How do we do it?" These differ from the prescriptive approach that begins with "This is . . ." and "Here's how . . ."

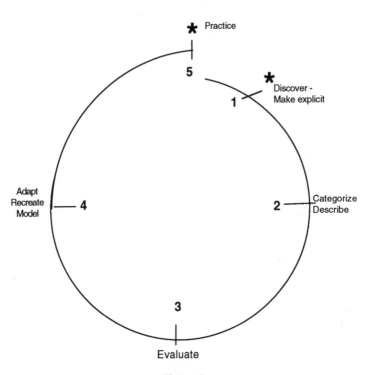

Figure 8
Key Steps in the Elicitive Model

For example, rather than preparing role plays for the training ahead of time, an elicitive approach posits that it is possible to invite participants in small groups to discuss real-life situations that involve them, and to subsequently use their description and presentation of the cases as raw material for discussion and the development of role plays in the course of the training. This simple shift places emphasis on the process of exploring their own situation, invites them to think through how it should be described, and often creates a sense of community as people share and recognize certain patterns and shared realities.

Naming and Categorizing.   Throughout the training process, serious effort is made to foster a level of innovation and creativity that permits participants to make explicit and take ownership in the approaches and models that emerge from their implicit understandings. The movement from implicit to explicit knowledge is discovery. Sustaining and making explicit a constructive social tool involves naming. However, unlike the prescriptive approach, the elicitive model does not provide names for tools and action. It rather encourages the participants to define and name their own understandings. This idea of course is not new. At the cutting edge of innovation in the field of conflict resolution, people are discovering and naming new processes, techniques, and models. Subsequently, those innovations are passed on as techniques but having eliminated the process of discovery and naming. What may be new in the elicitive approach is the guideline that discovery and naming are legitimate, possible, and necessary as training processes, processes that are both rooted in and dependent on the knowledge of people and that foster creativity and innovation.

As a step in the training process, this component represents the opportunity to identify and categorize more clearly the types of activity, approaches, and roles that are typical to how conflicts are handled in their setting. The effort here is descriptive in nature, permitting a process of naming and categorizing what is and not whether what it is works, is appropriate, or is desired.

Evaluation.   A third component involves the element of contextualized evaluation. Participants are invited not only to rediscover and describe what is present in their setting, but also to evaluate what helps and what does not. Contextualized evaluation simply means that participants in a given setting evaluate their own action and behavior according to the standards and values of that setting, rather than judging their approaches according to outside criteria. In other words, participants are afforded an opportunity to explore questions such as: "What is helpful and good that we do?" "What gets in the way?" "What do we lack?" "What needs to be changed?"

Adapt/Recreate.   A crucial step involves the adaptation and recreation of what exists toward what participants suggest as a more suited or desired modality of operation. Here, one may seek new ways of handling conflict, adapt old approaches into a new and evolving context, build on strengths, but change aspects that are weak. This step may well involve comparing and contrasting approaches coming from other settings and experimenting with how conflicts should be approached. What begins to emerge is their own model and proposals for application.

Practical application. Finally, the training process involves exercises and opportunities for experimenting with and refining the ideas, approaches, and models that emerge. Although this may initially take place through simulated application, practice of the model in real life is paramount involving the cycle of reflection and action. Freire (1970, 76) once wrote that humanity is not "built in silence, but in word, in work, in action-reflection." By this he is referring to the cycle that encourages the development of education based on discovery, naming, and application; then rediscovery, renaming, and reapplication.

In essence, the key to model application and development comes from the test of trying it out in real-life circumstances, then returning with experience to the process of description and evaluation. This process takes the training cycle a full circle but leaves the participants at a different place than where they began.

The goals of the elicitive process may include, but go beyond and are oriented toward, a different level than the mastery of technique. The approach underscores that training, like the practice of conflict resolution and mediation, is participatory and circular. Its primary goals are empowerment through self and context awareness and creation of appropriate models of conflict resolution. Empowerment in the training process is understood as validating and building on the strengths and promise of resources from within a context rather than from outside. Training is thus based on a participatory design for creating appropriate models of conflict transformation.

The methodology, based heavily on a problem-posing approach, pushes out these goals. The training format is understood as a catalyst. By catalyst, I refer to exercises and inputs aimed at creating an encounter between participants and their knowledge of conflict in their setting. Natural in-setting resources, such as everyday language, proverbs, and current situations and problems, are sought as windows and raw material for stimulating the knowledge. Role plays, for example, are not used primarily as a device to master a technique or process, but rather to discover and subsequently name the approach emerging from participants' natural way of thinking about and responding to situations. The trainer's role is to help facilitate that encounter and the ongoing innovation that emerges.

Conclusion

In summary, our purpose here was to outline the key elements and characteristics of the elicitive training approach. The overview suggests that this approach is not based on transferring knowledge from trainer to participant, but rather on building and creating models from an interaction among participants themselves and with the trainer. The overall approach to training, rather than depending on the trainer as expert, draws a closer parallel from facilitation of an encounter in which leaders help participants create their own learning environment and develop models for dealing with conflict. Thus, the base of the pure elicitive approach does not lie with a series of techniques to be mastered by the trainee, but rather in the shift in relationship between participants and trainer that redefines expertise as implicit in the setting rather than in the trainer, and redefines power as participation in discovery and naming rather than transfer of knowledge.

Fundamentally, the elicitive approach builds from knowledge in a setting, and thus, unlike the prescriptive approach, it cannot bracket culture. Culture, in other words, natural and taken-for-granted knowledge in a given setting, is understood as the foundation and seedbed of model development and creation. This brief conclusion leads to a more detailed comparison of the prescriptive and elicitive models.

7

Prescriptive and Elicitive
The Critical Tension

I f I have learned anything through the years of working across very diverse settings, it is a respect for both the importance and complexity of culture. In the preceding two chapters, I outlined the key characteristics of two different pure-type approaches to training. In my own cross-cultural work, I have experienced a slow and sometimes painful process of self-awareness in regard to how much a prescriptive modality has dominated my training style. My challenge has been not only to recognize when and where that approach is useful, and where it has been inappropriate, but also to learn to work at moving down the spectrum toward the elicitive approach and at broadening my training repertoire. I refer to this movement as developing an elicitive-oriented approach to training. With this orientation I recognize a critical tension that lies between the self-confidence and experience I have in working with conflict in my home setting—often classified as expertise—and the ultimate goal of empowerment of others and development of appropriate models of conflict resolution in other cultural contexts.

The purpose of this chapter is to provide a comparison of the prescriptive and elicitive models. In building these models, I have suggested that they represent typifications on extreme ends of a spectrum and not exact descriptions of actual training practice. In real life, any given training inevitably has some elements of both. However, setting up the spectrum and comparing these models help us to identify a number of key aspects about how we approach both training and the complex issue of culture (see figure 9).

Comparing the Models

There are numerous areas where the differences between the two models emerge with clarity. Each of these could well merit a detailed explanation; however, the purpose here is to provide a summary, highlighting the key distinctions, as laid out in figure 9.

In the prescriptive model, training is conducted on the basis of transfer, of passing on to the participants the approach, strategy, and technique mastered by the trainer. The event itself is built around providing, teaching, and learning a specific model of conflict resolution. The elicitive approach, on the other hand, undertakes training as an opportunity and an encounter for participants in a given setting to discover and create models of conflict resolution in the context of their setting. This fundamental difference in how training is understood and approached creates a number of distinct features in the two models.

The guiding framework for the prescriptive approach lies in the how to's, in other words, in providing recipes suggesting how conflict and its management ought to be pursued. The guiding elicitive framework is constructed around the what do's, in providing a process for people to engage what they know and build from that knowledge.

Thus, in the elicitive model, the participants and the knowledge they bring about conflict in their setting are a significant resource in the training. The prescriptive approach, however, underscores the centrality of the trainer's models and knowledge. In this latter instance, training is content-oriented, with the express purpose of having the participants master the approach and techniques. The trainer plays out the role of expert, providing a model for how the technique works and facilitating the event. The elicitive model is process oriented, providing an opportunity for

PRESCRIPTIVE <————————————————————> ELICITIVE

Training as transfer	Training as discovery and creation
Resource: Model and knowledge of trainer	Resource: Within-setting knowledge
Training as content oriented: Master approach and technique	Training as process oriented: Participate in model creation
Empowerment as learning new ways and strategies for facing conflict	Empowerment as validating and building from context
Trainer as expert, model, and facilitator	Trainer as catalyst and facilitator
Culture as technique	Culture as foundation and seedbed

Figure 9

Prescriptive/Elicitive: A Comparative Summary

people to participate in model discovery and creation. The trainer constructs a role of catalyst and facilitator.

Both models can create dynamic education to empower people, but do so from a different basis. The prescriptive approach empowers participants inasmuch as they learn and master new ways, techniques, and strategies for facing and handling conflict. The elicitive pursues empowerment as validating and building from resources that are present in the setting.

Training and Culture

Particularly crucial to the broader discussion in this book are the points of view these models embody with respect to the role and place of culture. Succinctly, the prescriptive approach sees culture as technique. The elicitive understands culture as a seedbed and as a foundation. Both perspectives merit further exploration.

There are two levels at which the prescriptive approach understands culture as technique. At one level, prescription assumes a certain amount of universality. The model is transfer-based: knowledge and experience that has emerged from and has been applied in a particular cultural context is now moving to another. The premise of universality not only suggests that such a transfer can successfully take place across lines of culture, class, and context but further that the techniques are culturally neutral. Participants who learn the basic components and techniques involved in the model can and will adapt them to meet their particular cultural context and needs. At a second level, the prescriptive approach sees culture itself as an area of advanced training. Here, practitioners already trained in the basic model receive advanced levels of skill training related to culture. This training is often reduced to short recipes: How to recognize cultural differences, how to work with a given ethnic group, or how to negotiate effectively across cultures.[1]

In these approaches, culture is understood primarily as a special area of technique, an assumption that makes few if any provisions for two key factors. First, such a transfer can easily sidestep the resources available in a given context by embracing those coming from outside the setting. And second, the working assumption that the incoming model is culturally neutral and applicable across contexts is taken at face value. In fact, the incoming model is embedded with culture, but is rarely recognized as such.

For example, if I use a prescriptive approach to teach Hondurans how to do neighborhood mediation, based on my experiences in Virginia, my model will carry implicit cultural assumptions common to a Virginia setting. These assumptions will affect how participants see the role of the third parties and conflictants; the pace, purpose, and style of communication; and the purpose of the resolution process—to name a few. I will likely also make more concrete cultural assumptions in terms of specific conflict-resolution techniques that are fundamental to the implementation of the model we use in Virginia. For example, conflictants may be expected to be autonomous decision-makers, who can openly and directly talk about their problems and negotiate an agreement in a two-hour "session" in my office.

1. An overview of these training approaches is delineated in an interview with Dianne LeResche and Jennifer Spruill in the *Conciliation Quarterly*, 9, no. 1 (Winter 1990).

Given a fundamental proclivity toward technique skill development in most trainings, many of the techniques will be based on suggestions evolving around language and communication patterns common to the Virginia setting, for example. In a pure prescriptive approach, I would likely use role plays developed around typical cases I have experienced in Virginia, which are useful for highlighting aspects of the process or practicing the model. Each and every one of these aspects of training include implicit cultural assumptions, which are often appropriate and helpful to a particular sociolinguistic context and community, but are foreign and may even be counterproductive in others.

In sum, prescription suggests universality of technique. Transfer into different cultural contexts is accomplished through model adjustments or minimization of the relative importance of cultural boundedness in the proposed model to be transferred.

On the other side, the elicitive approach does not see culture as an element to be added as a further level of technique, or as a challenging complication to which techniques must be adapted. Cultural context and knowledge about conflict-in-setting make up the foundation through which the model development happens. Participants' natural knowledge, their way of being and doing, their immediate situation, their past heritage, and their language are seen as the seedbed in which the training and model building will be rooted. Validating and exciting these cultural elements as resources is the fundamental goal of the training endeavor.

However, an elicitive approach held in its pure form may miss many important cross-cultural points of contact and fertilization. If we restrict outside contact and exchange, then the process of training minimizes learning and limits the education into a narrow field of exploration. After all, people are interested in and attend trainings precisely because they want to move beyond current practices. Cross-cultural and cross-experience exchanges are among the richest and most beneficial ways that people learn and expand. What is crucial in maintaining empowerment is a high view of participants being provided a voice and the power to evaluate and decide, which ultimately is rooted in their understanding of themselves and their own setting.

Conclusion

This comparative overview has suggested key aspects of the prescriptive and elicitive approaches to conflict resolution training. Both of these models have strengths and weaknesses. The prescriptive approach is based on teaching a model that has emerged from considerable experience and knowledge the trainer brings from real life. The model has demonstrated itself to be both operative and useful in a given setting and perhaps in multiple settings. The techniques provide concrete ideas and skills, and move the participants toward application, often with a keen sense of accomplishment and empowerment. The prescriptive approach can be compacted and may take relatively little time to pass on and accomplish goals of preparing participants for application.

On the downside, as delineated above, the assumptions of cultural universality that underlie the prescriptive approach do not always hold. In fact, what becomes universal may be the homogenization of people to fit into the approach. The prescriptive model also sends the subtle messages that the trainer's ways are best, that resources for empowerment lie outside the setting, and that productive conflict resolution—like other models of development—lies with emulating those who have made more "progress." This concern becomes all the more important when the trainer and the trainer's model emerge from a dominant culture—white, anglo, middle-class, academic, urban, western, modern, industrialized—but are applied in nondominant settings.

The strength of the elicitive approach is its diligence in respecting and building from the cultural context, in fostering participatory design, and in constructing appropriate models in the setting. It places emphasis on participants designing, discovering together, and naming the conflict resolution models that emerge. This approach understands its role in a longer time frame and sees the use of culture as a resource rather than as the short-term transfer of technique or adaption of models to a cultural setting.

In its pure form, however, the elicitive approach takes time and involves considerable commitment. The proposed outcomes are not easily measured, and the creation process can often be painful. The elicitive approach does not provide formulas or answers. The ambiguity of discovering and then moving toward application can produce a sense of frustration and impatience. Further, if held in its pure form, it may unnecessarily minimize comparison and contrast with other settings denying participants important learning and growth opportunities.

Although we set out to describe two ideal types of training, I believe that the mainstream of conflict resolution training, particularly mediation, is closer to the prescriptive than to the elicitive end of the spectrum, even though many of the training events take place in culturally, economically and linguistically diverse settings.

This comparative framework provides us with some elements useful for a critique of current conflict resolution training practices as they relate to the issue of culture; however, that is not the exclusive purpose of this essay. Rather, it is my intent to use the creative tension inherent in the framework to provide a handle for exploring the potential of an elicitive approach and how it changes our thinking about training, relationships, and intervention. Moving toward the elicitive model suggests the need for critical reflection about what we are moving away from—in this instance, transfer-based training in cross-cultural settings.

Let me make this case by returning to the framework for building peace outlined in the second chapter. I believe that framework invites us to critical reflection not only on the content of what we teach but also on the method by which we teach it. As the conflict resolution field has grown in popularity in recent years and has begun to carve out a professional niche in North America, we need to raise the question of whether training is approached primarily as a question of professional and technical expansion, over and above the project of promoting a movement for social empowerment and transformation. Although these are not necessarily incompatible, I believe that as opportunities have emerged in other cultural settings, we have too easily assumed that our approach to conflict resolution is technically transferable and have thus, so to say, put all our eggs in the basket of developing and mastering the transfer of conflict resolution knowledge and technique.

My own position is that most trainings provided in diverse cultural settings would benefit from a combination of the two approaches. On the one hand, accumulated expertise and knowledge about approaches to conflict and its transformation—knowledge that stands at the base of the prescriptive approach—is an invaluable resource in working with others. Undeniably, as far as I know, people learn by experiencing new approaches, and they can often reflect more clearly and constructively on their models through a process of comparison and contrast. In fact, the pattern distinguished in social history is one in which the meeting and interaction of cultures produces change and growth. However, when a given approach to conflict is presented as the model, and when no efforts are made to build from the context and cultural resources in a setting, the very strength of the expertise becomes its main weakness, dominated by a narrow vision and even arrogance. On the other hand, respecting people and their knowledge and encouraging them to look for answers within themselves and within their context—the essence of the elicitive approach—are crucial aspects of building appropriate models and longterm sustainability. Yet if the elicitive approach adapts a purist stance that does not encourage comparison, does not share full knowledge of others' approaches and ideas, it can be disempowering and narrow in the opposite direction, by keeping people ignorant.

My experience has suggested the need to expand my repertoire and capacities on the elicitive side. In many ways, the key to movement toward an elicitive approach is not as much a change in training content as it is a change in relationship between trainer and participant. It invites us to move away from the residue of imperialism embedded in the prescriptive framework—subtle as it often is—and toward a relationship of social and cultural empowerment based on mutuality and respect. Such transformative movement is never easy nor necessarily clear. It is a little like Gandhi's depiction of nonviolence as a story of experiments with Truth.

Up to this point in the book, I have presented primarily analytical and at times abstract descriptions of these models. In the final section, I will share some of my experiments with the elicitive-oriented approach, which will flesh out through stories and concrete examples how I have slowly made the journey to expand the repertoire of training capacity.

PART THREE

Experiments in Elicitive Training

8

Language and Metaphor as Natural Resources in Conflict Training

Thus far we have outlined a theoretical framework for analyzing approaches to conflict resolution training. Now, we shift to practical and concrete examples of how an elicitive approach to training can be pursued. I will use examples drawn primarily from training experiences emerging from workshop or seminar formats. These events tended to be short term; however, in at least one project, I had the opportunity of working with a group for a full year, meeting twice weekly. Here, the elicitive framework was explored in terms of identifying needs, developing learning and action projects, and putting into practice concrete models for intervention. This event took place in Puntarenas, Costa Rica, under the auspices of the Ministry of Justice and the University for Peace. The experiments and projects of that year were compiled in a history of the training project written by the participants, which is available through the Ministry of Education in Costa Rica (Kavanaugh 1989). In this section, I will concentrate primarily on how I have endeavored to tap cultural knowledge as a resource for constructing appropriate models of conflict resolution in the context of a workshop. This chapter focuses on language and metaphor as natural resources.

Images and Synonyms of Conflict

An early part in many seminars on mediation and conflict resolution is a discussion of what constitutes conflict and how it works. Often, a definition is provided. Invariably in my experience, if one is not provided someone will ask that one be given. Most trainers have a preferred definition, from among the many, that outlines the key patterns and dynamics characterizing conflict. We rarely notice that the term "conflict" tends to be a buzz word used by academicians or professionals in the field and that it is quite abstract and general. In real life, the term itself is rarely used in everyday parlance, although there are a hundred common ways of saying it. I became much more aware of this as I crossed cultural and language boundaries. Suddenly the common ways of saying conflict were no longer common nor known to me. In fact, they were at times novel and surprising, and sometimes even totally beyond my comprehension.

I remember an enlightening conversation I had one evening in Puntarenas, with one of the participants in our workshop, about a neighborhood problem. They were in a real *clavo*, a nail, she explained. After she had finished, I remarked that people in Puntarenas do not frequently use the word conflict to describe these situations. "Ah no," she replied, "here we do not have conflicts. Conflicts are what they have in Nicaragua. In Puntarenas we have *pleitos, lios,* and *enredos* (fights, messes, and entanglements)." She meant specifically that conflict refers to wars, which at the time Nicaragua was experiencing but Costa Rica was not. She had "hit the nail on the head," so to speak. Indeed, there was an entire repertoire of terms and phrases describing the many faces of conflict, a wealth of terminology, common to them but unknown to me. Curious about this language and convinced that it represented an unmined resource, I began to collect words and phrases that were used as popular slang and descriptors of conflict. In Central America, my collection grew to more than 200 Spanish words. These words and their accompanying metaphors created many hours of discussion and enormous insight into how people think about, respond to, and experience conflict in their everyday setting.

Everyday Language as a Training Resource

I pushed my curiosity into a training process. Rather than initiating a seminar with a definition, I would often start by asking participants to gather in small groups and list everyday words and phrases synonymous with or closely related to conflict. After thirty minutes we would compile a single list in the plenary session building from all the groups. In Central America, these terms could vary from "eggplant" and "hot as a pig's blood" to being "carried off by a mule" or "bit by a witch." I have been surprised time and again how a group of people divided into six small groups can come up with sixty to eighty terms in an hour-long exercise.

Discussion then ensued around the dominant images people have of conflict, the categories that their languages create for understanding it, and the meaning of certain terms and phrases. Where a longer process was possible, each of the words or phrases was written on a single index card, in a process similar to story boarding. The cards were then arranged, like pieces in a puzzle, according to commonality of meaning, in groups or by levels, permitting people to create a popular understanding of conflict based on natural language.

For example, in the course of about five meetings the group in Puntarenas arranged more than eighty common sayings and words into a complex set of relationships and dynamics (Lederach 1986). They saw their terminology as describing the situation externally and internally as well as describing the individual and the actions taken. In each of these categories, the terms expressed the rising intensity through various levels, from "entanglements" to "nails" to "fights" to "violent brawls." Key metaphors revolved around heat, feeling trapped or lost with no way out, and understanding conflict as embedded in a network of people. In the end, the exercise provided much more than a definition. It opened a window into common language and knowledge as a base for understanding themselves and their views of conflict.

Short of this more extensive exercise, many words or phrases can be identified that capture metaphoric images and insights directly related to the experience of conflict. Language is always more than a vehicle for communication. It is also a window into how people organize both their understanding and expression of conflict, often in keeping with cultural patterns and ways of operating. Lakoff and Johnson (1980) suggest that metaphors are an inherent feature of how people organize and give meaning to situations. Hocker and Wilmot (1991) push that more directly in terms of conflict, proposing that metaphors can be used as tools for analysis in intervention and consulting. I have found that these common, everyday terms, an integral part of local vocabulary, provide significant insight into both the experience of conflict and the potential identification of models for how it can appropriately be approached and handled in that setting. Let me give several examples.

In one exercise in Mexico, with a group of about thirty participants, more than ninety words and phrases were identified. In the follow-up discussion I asked whether any of the words stood out with special significance. One person almost immediately suggested that the word *desmadre* represented in a nutshell the Mexican experience of conflict. This was a term that I had heard quite often in Spain, but not as much in Central America. It translates as disorder or chaos, but literally means to be "without a mother." In the course of discussion, we probed not only the images and meanings of chaos and disorder, but the more profound significance of mother, of her role in the family in maintaining stability, of mothers as peacemakers.

At one level, the exercise could end here, as a look at an interesting word. At another level, we can push it out and see it as a window into ourselves, as a resource for how we think and act. For example, the metaphor of *desmadre* as conflict is not the absence of father, but the more total and devastating disintegration that emerges without mother. Practically, it begins to raise a more explicit understanding of the central role of women in the resolution of family conflict in Latin America. It highlights the significance of women's natural networks as a resource for handling conflicts and women's key conciliatory role of holding people together. Such insights are important at both a conceptual (conflict resolution as restoration and holding people together as opposed to problem solving) and a practical level (how information travels, who people go to for help, who has the trust and responsibility).

Take a second example. During a workshop with appropriate technology, health, and community leaders in Guatemala, an interesting discussion emerged around how people responded to conflictive situations. All of the people present were from various indigenous communities in the highlands of Guatemala. All had lost close friends and relatives in the struggle of recent years, and most of them were under considerable daily pressure. One of the phrases for conflict they identified was a common expression known in much of Latin America, "the Indian came out of me." I asked one of the participants, who had used that phrase, how he understood it and what it meant. As I recall, he explained that he had to avoid conflict because his emotions were too close to the surface. "If I let myself go," he explained, "I could lose it. I could explode. The Indian would come out, and I would regret it."

We spent some time that afternoon exploring the metaphor. The phrase is often used precisely in the way this native health promoter had explained. "The Indian comes out" characterizes situations where things deteriorate to explosive fighting. However, the metaphor also carries an historic, imperial projection. The discussion suggested that the phrase is built on images of civilization and savagery. To move toward civilization is good. To move toward the Indian is bad. The Indian cannot control himself or herself. In essence, they concluded, to be civil means to keep the Indian in check. The thought arose that what might be needed was for the Indian to come out. The simple, common phrase became a resource, not only at the level of how we respond to conflict, but as a significant window into the situation and our part in it.

A third example emerges from perhaps the most common and significant synonym of conflict in Central American in the word *enredo*, or as it is often used, *estamos bien enredados*. "We are all entangled." A simple translation does not do justice to the metaphoric image of this understanding of conflict. *Enredo* is a fishing metaphor at its roots. It is built around the Spanish word, *red*, a fisherman's net. To be *enredado* is to be tangled, caught in a net. The image is one of knots and connections: an intimate and intricate mess. A net, when tangled, must be worked through and undone slowly and patiently. Even untangled, it still remains connected and knotted; it is a whole. A net is also frequently torn, leaving holes that must be sewn back together, knotting once again the separated loose ends. In other words, *enredo* is a concept of conflict as embedded in tight-knit, primary social relationships. The image is indicative of how people think and respond to conflict in Central America, as emerging and being handled in the networking of relationships.

Notice how this simple metaphor begins to open doors about approaches to conflict. Rather than driven by individualism and autonomous thinking (often reflective of how we in North America reduce interpersonal conflict to the key individuals), an *enredo* conceptualization thinks of extended families and key friendships. Rather than looking for neutral outsiders to serve as mediators, an *enredo* perspective looks to my own network for key people who also know the person with whom I have the problem. Rather than isolating and resolving issues, an *enredo* view understands "holding us together" as the key element. Each of these perspectives suggests the cultural bases of how conflict is understood, what models might be suggested for approaching it, and how third parties are appropriately drawn in and involved.

Proverbs and Storytelling

I have also found that proverbs can serve as an interesting window into how people understand and work with conflict. This is especially true in cultural settings like Africa, or more specifically, in an oral tradition like that of Somalia, for example, where drawing on wisdom and oratory skills is both a revered art and a conflict-resolution tool (Samatar 1982).[1] There are several levels where proverbs can prove useful.[2]

---

1. At a very broad level, proverbs are linked to an advice-giving mode of conflict resolution, which I think is practically quite different than a facilitating modality of conflict resolution. An elicitive approach, rather than assuming a value judgement about advice giving, will look to proverbial wisdom and approaches seeking to maximize their inherent resource and modality.
2. Both of David Augsburger's (1986, 1991) books on cross-cultural counseling and mediation provide extensive and helpful surveys of traditional wisdom and proverbs.

First, any given proverb carries with it certain images and suggestions. Many are directly related to conflict and what to do about
it; others make references to traditional ways of understanding process. It is interesting that our modern, technical talk about conflict
is also imbued with key images. In mediation and diplomacy, for
example, the peacemaking process revolves around images of
order and organization best described both literally and metaphorically as the "table." It is very natural for me to describe mediation
as creating an acceptable table or getting people to sit down at a
table and work things out. What perhaps goes unnoticed are the
implicit characteristics of the table as a peacemaking image, especially in diplomacy. It suggests an emphasis on rationalism, formal
specialized roles, meeting indoors, and bureaucracy.

Compare that with a proverb from East Africa, which says,
"What old people see seated at the base of the tree, young people
cannot see from the branches." On the surface, the immediate message emphasizes the wisdom of age as a resource for seeing things
and understanding. It points to the traditional use of elders as a
resource in conflict resolution. At another level, however, we tap
into important conceptual metaphors underpinning the cultural
and social organization of conflict resolution. The images in the
proverb are of outdoor, community space, of the use of a local resource and traditional forum for handling community problems.
The tree is a place for people to gather. In fact, certain trees may
hold special significance for a given tribe, representing a space that
organizes their conflict resolution activity, connecting them to
peacemaking tasks, to each other, and to their environment.
Such a space suggests a process of conflict resolution based on
face-to-face relations, worked out through informal, oral, and
nonbureaucratic procedures and settings.

Second, one of the biggest challenges of proverb use is know-
ing how to employ proverbial wisdom as a confrontational and
conflict resolution tool. I have sat through some long and ardu-
ous debates between Somalis, where a particular proverb emerges
to make a point. It is then countered with a second proverb pushing the exact opposite idea. The revered art is how to frame and
present the specific concerns in the debate.

The challenge becomes clear in using proverbs to respond to
actual conflict. For example, a Tswana saying suggests "the

solution to a problem lies with more talk." On the other hand, an Ethiopian ambassador discussing possible negotiations to end the war in the late 1980s once quoted a traditional wisdom saying, "When the knees get weak the tongue gets long," suggesting that only the weak negotiate. From one vantage point, proverbs provide contradictory advice and may appear superficial. However, from a different angle, proverbs as traditional wisdom can be seen as a flexible tool representing a repertoire of sayings for responding to the many faces of conflict.

Taking this latter view, I developed an exercise with proverbs for exploring differences in how individuals approach conflict (Lederach 1986). I put together some twenty Spanish proverbs, common to most people in Latin America, and suggesting very different ways of responding to conflict, from going along and not disrupting, to seeking a half-way point, to avoiding. The exercise was a more contextualized way of getting at conflict styles, but one based on natural knowledge that brought out what people knew about themselves and their setting.

At yet another level, I have found that many proverbs suggest fundamental strategies about conflict that are not easily conveyed in a more cognitive mode. An example of this comes from working across cultures with the now widely known text *Getting to Yes* (Fisher and Ury 1981). It has been translated into a number of languages, including Spanish. In the book, there is a strategy for dealing with difficult or powerful people. The strategy is known as BATNA—the Best Alternative to a Negotiated Agreement. In many conflict resolution and mediation training seminars, this term has become common parlance. "If you cannot get realistic flexibility from a disputant," we say, "have them consider their BATNA."

The translation in the Spanish version of Fisher and Ury's book created an equally odd acronym, MAAN—Mejor alternativa a un acuerdo negociado. For many of the people I worked with at grassroots levels, this was difficult if not impossible to understand cognitively, much less to use practically.[3] It simply rang of

3. The book is published by CECSA, Mexico City, Mexico, under the title *Obtenga el Sí: El arte de negociar sin ceder*, 1984.

sophistication, complexity, and professional technique, something "foreign." However, the same idea is present, and has been for generations, in the form of many well-known Spanish proverbs that we know in English as the choice between the lesser of two evils. For example, in Spanish they say, "Salad is better than nothing." "Better to walk with a limp than not at all." "A bird in hand is worth more than one hundred flying." The fundamental idea of these proverbs is to compare situations and opt for what takes us closer to our goal or what we need. An elicitive-oriented approach, using these proverbs, would attempt to discover and work from what is natural and available in the cultural framework rather than attempting, as a starting point, to transfer the concept wrapped in its technical jargon from another setting. In this particular instance, using well-known proverbial wisdom of comparing outcomes in order to make choices provides a useful vehicle for conveying a concept as opposed to teaching people a new language. Working from common knowledge and understanding moves us away from seeing the concept or skill as something new we have to learn, to something we knew and can now apply in a new way.

Finally, these cognitive and metaphoric ways of perceiving the world also subtly permeate our models of intervening in conflict. This phenomenon was most evident to me when I found myself mediating in Central American conflicts. Why is it, I asked myself, that in the middle of listening to someone give their side of a problem I have a natural inclination to make a list, to break their story down into parts such as issues and concerns? But, when I ask them about issues, they seem to have a natural inclination to tell me yet another story. The difference, I think, lies in the distinction between analytical and holistic thinking. Our North American conflict resolution approaches are driven by analysis; that is, the breaking of things down into their component parts. Storytelling, on the other hand—by which I mean recounting what happened by providing proverbs, analogies, or even fables—keeps all the parts together. It understands problems and events as a whole.

Increasingly, I have become interested in the role of storytelling, of using analogies and fables, not only as illustrative of points about a technique that one may wish to emphasize in a

training, but also as direct tools of intervention. What I recall from
my early training experiences and seminars are the stories trainers told about their experiences. However, to see and understand
story as a tool of pedagogy and intervention takes a shift in thinking. The shift moves us away from understanding storytelling as
less serious because it feels like play time. It propels us toward
the view that stories create a holistic approach to thinking and
understanding in which people are invited to mingle with the
characters as a device of interacting with their own realities. This
view in fact has become a central feature of recent developments
in family systems practice. Edwin Friedman, for example, argues
that playfulness and fables are as crucial to the therapeutic process as the more serious work of cognitive analysis (Friedman 1985
and 1990). Peggy Pabt also worked extensively with the use of
metaphors and imaging in the family therapy process (Walters et
al. 1988). It would seem that a cutting edge of North American
psychiatry and problem solving is circling back to what traditional
wisdom has known all along.

Conclusion

As a way of concluding, let me tell a little anecdote. In the
year-long training project in Costa Rica, one of the oldest participants was a great-grandmother, Doña Fidelia. She came from one
of the local "invasions," referring to landless people who together
occupy a parcel of land owned by someone far more wealthy, who
usually lives in the capital. Doña Fidelia had lived through three
separate invasions. She was now the head of an extended family
that included her ailing mother, several of her children, and a fair
number of grandchildren. She was attending the course along with
two of her sons.

About halfway through the year, the group decided that each
meeting would be facilitated by members of the group on a ro-
tating basis. Several weeks later, Doña Fidelia told me that she felt
she needed to quit the group. I was very disappointed because of
her significant insights into community and family problems, even
though she always saw them as "stuff anybody knows."

"Why do you feel you cannot go on?" I asked.

"Well, Don Juan Pablo," she replied, in her usual respectful way and after considerable conversation, "I cannot read or write, and will not be able to lead the group."

Pounded in through the years had been this message of what was needed to be someone, to count, to lead. There may have been no one else in the group who was better prepared or more experienced in dealing with family problems and land invasions than this woman. Yet she was blocked by her own view of herself. The most crucial aspect of empowerment is to move from "I cannot" to "I can."

"You know," I replied to Doña Fidelia, "leading a group is a lot like being a grandmother." Our conversation went on. Although she never formally led the group, she stayed as a valued grandmother, as trusted a peacemaker as you can get in that setting.

You may draw multiple points from the story. Mine parallels the point made by Milton Erikson in reference to reframing in psychotherapy. "Take what the patient is bringing you," he writes. "This rule stands in sharp contrast to the teaching of most schools of psychotherapy, which either tend to apply mechanically one and the same procedure to the most disparate patients, or find it necessary first to teach the patient a new language, and then to attempt change by communicating in this language. By contrast, reframing presupposes that the therapist learn the patient's language, and this can be done much more quickly and economically than the other way around" (Watzlawick et al. 1978, 104).

The elicitive-oriented approach is built on drawing out and using what people bring you, even when it is not understood by them as a resource. It looks for natural language as a tool for learning, teaching, and naming. Much more than simple communication or interesting differences, it understands language, metaphor, proverb, and story as resources, mechanisms, and approaches to conflict resolution.

9

So to Whom Do You Turn?
Discovery and Creation of Mediation Models

I have described in some detail the philosophical roots and goals of an elicitive approach to training, but the question still remains of how exactly you accomplish these ideals. A familiar saying in Spanish suggests that "Between what is said and what is done there runs a deep chasm." In other words, in real life it is never easy to fully accomplish the ideals and goals we set for ourselves. Specific to our concerns here, the elicitive format suggests that it should be possible to build a model of mediation through a training experience. In the next two chapters, I will present several approaches and exercises within an elicitive perspective aimed specifically at model building in mediation. First, I outline a training process that builds from people's natural understanding of providing help. In the following chapter, I suggest how role-play can be used as a tool for developing mediation models.

Seeking Help: An Elicitive Exercise

In many introductory workshops in North American mediation, training begins with an overview and description of the process. The format is often a short descriptive lecture about the purpose, structure, rules, expectations, and roles that comprise the mediation process. Implicit in the opening description are the cultural assumptions of how the process is accomplished and the naming of the process and its components. In settings where I work with groups from cultural and linguistic contexts other than my own, I have used a different opening exercise, one that takes several steps back from presenting a process or naming it. It is built around three key questions. It can be used as a shorter introductory piece or can easily provide the material for a longer, more exploratory effort. The exercise follows these steps for setup and implementation.

1. Open the exercise with a statement like this: "I want everyone to think back to a time when you found yourself experiencing problems with someone else. You know things are not right. This can be a problem in your family, among friends, at work, or in your neighborhood. Now, I want you to think through this question. If things got difficult and you felt you needed help with this problem, who would you go to for help? Get the image of this person or persons in your mind. Then work on and share the following with your small group: Why did you choose this person? What characteristics does he or she have? What do you expect from this person?"

2. Invite participants to think on their own for a short while and then to join a small group. These groups discuss their various answers and compile a list of ideas to report back to the large group.

3. Record the responses on a blackboard, on newsprint, or on index cards. Index cards are most useful if a longer exploratory process is desired. In the process of reporting, people are encouraged to talk about examples of what they mean or why they chose a certain concept or characteristic. As the responses come out, ideas that are repeated are marked or noted.

4. The final step moves toward a summary and conclusion, the detail of which varies with the time and purpose of the exercise. For example, if time is limited and the exercise is proposed as an initial step leading to more exploration of real life cases, summarize the emerging major themes by building from the key and repeated ideas. On the other hand, if time permits, it can be a very

useful exercise to ask the participants to create their own interpretation and even the beginnings of a model. In this case, we
might follow the storyboarding process.

Storyboarding in Model Creation

Walt Disney developed the process of storyboarding in outlining and producing cartoons. It has made its way into conflict
resolution as a useful process for identifying problems and possible solutions. I have been using a variation of storyboarding in
training as a tool for facilitating the discovery and creation of mediation models that may be implicit in the culture. In essence, the
storyboarding process involves working with index cards. A single
idea, word, or image is written on each card related to a given
theme. A story is then created by linking and grouping these cards
together by commonality or sequence. To create a mediation
model, I have used the process in the following format:

1. First, the most significant and key ideas identified in the
plenary sharing related to the three questions on seeking help are
written, one per index card.

2. A complete set of these index cards is given back to each
small working group.

3. Each group then works with the cards, almost as if they
formed a puzzle, reflecting on questions such as: How do these
ideas fit together? Is there a sequence? Are some ideas describing
a particular aspect of providing help? What would we call this
set of ideas or this aspect?

4. Each group then reports back on how it has arranged the
cards and ideas and is asked, among other things, to name the
key commonalities, or steps, or overall arrangements that have
been identified.

At each step in this process, we can push out the purpose of
the exercise as it relates to the objectives of an elicitive approach.
First, rather than describing a predefined process, participants are
invited to move back into their own experiences and identifying
the elements that are relevant in seeking and providing help.

Second, as trainers, we move away from the temptation of
naming the process or elements. The exercise tries to keep names
generic and general, such as "help" rather than "mediation."

Participants are the ones who provide concepts or categories that describe this help.

Third, the direction a training may go is never predictable. Many people will begin their reflection by saying, "it depends": "It depends whether I have an economic problem, or a family problem, or problem with my boss." On the surface, this may seem to be distracting. From the elicitive viewpoint, however, this is precisely the implicit knowledge that leads to explicit identification and appropriate model building. For example, in Uganda, one participant noted that if there were a problem with my brother we would go to my father or an uncle, but if the problem is with a neighbor, then we may need to seek out an elder. What begins to emerge are the ways people think about conflict, the resources and traditions they are intuitively aware of, why those are appropriate, and why they may no longer exist or are not used.

Fourth, working from a small group back to a larger group enhances the richness and the realism of what is discussed. This undergirds the proposition that people from the setting are not only the best resource for coming up with ideas about how things work; but they are also the best resource for providing a realistic check about whether an idea is valid.

Finally, especially if the longer process is followed, people can begin to push out key characteristics and ideas about how help is provided in their setting. Further steps often involve identifying obstacles, what things have been lost (for example, through modernization or immigration), what things hold promise that need to be worked on, and probably most importantly, what we call this process or processes. For example, in Panama among the Embere and Wounaan Indians, this early exercise resulted in the suggestion that providing help was a lot like guiding someone through the riverways of the dense jungle. For the remainder of our time we referred to third parties as guides.

An Example: Help in Central America

Because these descriptions and ideas appear somewhat abstract in the written form, let me describe several cases in Central America where time permitted us to look more carefully at the ideas. I have found that the questions—Who do you turn to? Why that person? What do you expect from them?—posed to different groups often identified a number of common words and themes. In a couple of cases, each of the words that came out more frequently in response to these questions was written on a card. People in smaller groups were then asked to take this set of cards—usually numbering between twenty and thirty—and arrange them accordingly to commonality, sequence, or whatever made most sense to them. On a number of occasions, the following kind of arrangement or conversation would emerge. For the benefit of the reader, I have placed quotation marks around words that emerged with frequency in the initial exercise.

First, key to why certain people are chosen were the ideas of "trustworthiness," that "we know them," that "they know us" and can "keep our confidences." These terms often came together in a single overarching concept: *confianza*, a profoundly cultural term that is inadequately translated as trust or confidence. In several groups, *confianza* became a key to understanding how they work at conflict and how they think about resolution and healing. *Confianza* points to relationship building over time, to a sense of "sincerity" a person has and a feeling of "security" the person "inspires" in us that we will "not be betrayed." *Confianza* is a key for "entry" into the problem and into the person with whom we have the problem. From the eyes of everyday experience in Central America, when I have a problem with someone I do not look for an outside professional. Rather I look for someone I trust who also knows the other person and is trusted by them. This kind of person can give "orientation" and "advice." Through this person, entry is accomplished.

Second, a number of terms often emerged around the idea of "support," "talk," and "listening." These almost always involved a popular term for an informal chat, *platicar*. This is more than simply "talking." It involves cultural understanding of communicative mechanisms for "sharing," "exchanging" and "checking things out." *Platicar* is fundamentally a way of being with another, of reaffirming the relationship, and in many more delicate situations of preparing the way for "dialogue" that may involve confrontation. Through the *platica* people feel "supported," "heard," "understood," and "accompanied."

Third, people want "help," "advice," and "direction." From others we seek "paths" that can lead us "out of the problem." Often, in working with the these words and concepts, two ideas stood out. First, was the concept of looking for or giving *consejo*, or advice. At a popular level, conflict resolution thinking is advice driven and sought. But it is not in the sense of giving advice that North American helping professions may advise against. Seeking and giving advice often has more to do with participation in seeking solution—in other words, brainstorming—than in narrowing to choose action or impose solution. Looking for advice is seeking the pool of collective wisdom, seeking support and understanding. Thus, in the course of a conversation, much advice may be batted around, providing the seeker with a sense of solidarity and ideas. Additionally, people often talked about the idea of *ubicarse*, which literally is to "locate oneself," or in our vernacular, "figuring out where I am." Getting advice, "identifying the problems," providing "orientation" are all part of figuring out what's going on, where I am, and where I should go.

Finally, a number of terms emerge around the concern of how I "get out" of this mess. People look for "solutions" most often understood as an *arreglo*, an "arrangement." This term combines a number of ideas, from "fixing things" and "putting things back together," to "getting an agreement" or "understanding." Key to an *arreglo* is a way of thinking that is holistic in nature, that is, seeing oneself and the problem in the context of a network rather than as isolated from it. Thus, an "arrangement" creates a *salida*, a common term meaning a way out, but a way out that maintains the network and relationship and fosters dignity. In other words, it saves face.

Pulling these ideas together, one group in Costa Rica outlined their understanding of how we get in and out of conflict and provide "help" by building on their terms as guidelines (see figure 10). It is worth noting that this overall outline resonates with important metaphors and images common to the way people think about conflict in a Central American setting. The language of conflict describes a journey involving the tasks of getting in, figuring

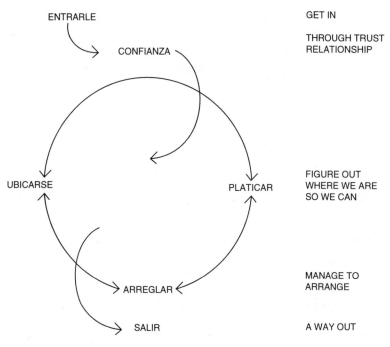

Figure 10
The Ins and Outs of Conflict Help in Central America

out where we are, and getting out. In fact, this set of concepts helps reinforce key cultural premises: a focus on relationship, trust-building, restoration of community, and use of people in the network. It focuses on being with others as a mode of restoration rather than applying technique as a mode of resolving problems.

In terms of model building, we are now in a position to take a further step. Each of these words—such as *confianza* or *arreglar*—has rich cultural and practical meaning and represents important organizing categories for model building. These common, everyday terms describing the action of working on the restoration of relationship and the resolution of conflict, renamed, become empowering tools. The model-building exercise rooted these words and processes within the culture and encouraged participants to name them, providing categories for further discovery, for exploration, and for use as the building blocks of a more explicit model.

Important questions can now guide the next steps in understanding more fully the applicability and implementation of the model: What are the approaches to building *confianza*? How does one pursue *la platica*? What are constructive elements for getting situated and arranging a way out?

Point of Convergence

The prescriptive-elicitive spectrum helps bring to the surface the question of cultural universality of conflict resolution and mediation practices. This question was posed in a sharper manner in a series of training workshops I conducted with the Northern Ireland Mediation Network. Having received early training in the North American mediation model, over the past years, community mediators in Northern Ireland have sought to "Irishize" the approach—creating a dilemma. In the Northern Ireland context, the early and current mediation training provided a vehicle of enrichment, a new way to look at and deal with conflict, which clearly created a sense of empowerment. Yet, the application of the training in real-life cases did not seem to bear the level of fruit expected in getting people into the process or carrying it to a successful mediated conclusion. People would come to trainings to learn models and skills, but the Irish people would not bring conflicts to be mediated along the lines proposed by the model. "How is it," I remember one participant asking, "that we can feel enlightened by learning the model and simultaneously uncomfortable that it does not quite fit?"

The question provided a rich and useful device for further exploration. In my analysis, it helped sharpen the underlying conviction that a convergence of universal and particular with prescriptive and elicitive was both possible and necessary. At a theoretical level, a heuristic framework was necessary, and at a training level a new tool was needed. These came together in what I consider to be one of the most basic of all sociological premises, that form follows function.

I would suggest we can bring the conflict functionalism of Coser (1956) together with a social constructionist view of Schutz (1967) and Blumer (1969). This is one way of looking at the seminal work of Gulliver (1979), who attempted broad case and cultural comparison in dispute resolution in order to establish the basic parameters of negotiation functions while recognizing the multiplicity of cultural forms. This approach was the general orientation of my early investigation into the cultural assumptions of the North American mediation model (1985), where I suggested mediation had a set of basic components that needed to be met, but that varied significantly in terms of the specific mechanisms for meeting them. Moving from function to form is like moving down a spectrum from universal to particular. As I outlined in chapter 5, the transfer modality in training rarely distinguishes analytically between these two. Most conflict-resolution and mediation training concentrates on "skills transfer," which are the more particular forms, as if the form was universal, when in fact the form tends to be more particular to the context and culture.

With this broad intuition in mind, over the course of the past year, I have devised and explored a training tool that suggests a convergence (figure 11). First developed in Spanish and shared in the Basque Country, and subsequently in Northern Ireland in early 1994, it remains in an experimental and rough form. It is built on four categories. *Facets* refers to basic aspects and components necessary for the work of any third-party process intervening in a social conflict. The *functions* respond to a set of key questions related to accomplishing the facets. The *forms* begin to answer the questions in terms of broader strategies and approaches, which are more culturally constructed for a given setting. The *formulas* are then seen as the specific tactics, skills, and mechanisms, or the technique, by which the forms are implemented.

The facet-function aspects suggest a series of things that will likely be dealt with in any mediated process. Based on earlier work and experience, I would outline these briefly as a circular, interactive process, although for purposes of analysis these appear as phases in figure 11.

Entry deals with the question of who will emerge as an acceptable third party and how the process and forum for dealing

UNIVERSAL <----- -----> PARTICULAR

		Community Mediation/U.S.		Somali Interclan Reconciliation	
FACET	FUNCTION	FORM	FORMULA	FORM	FORMULA
1. Entry	* Who? How? * Locate acceptable 3rd party * Seek help/remedy * Define process * Establish expectations	* Mediator/formal role * Face-to-face meeting with disputants	* Contact office * Introduction of process * Ground rules: roles/process * Sessions at office (2 hr) * Create trust/atmosphere of safety	* Prepare guurti * Elders councils * Traditional authority	* Early contact/women to clan of origin * Intra-sub-clan deliberations * Establish space for dialogue (stop killings)

2. Gather Perspectives	* What happened?
	 * Create forum/process
	 * Express conflict/vent
	 * Acknowledge
	   * Grievances
	   * Feelings
	   * Experiences
	   * Concerns
		* Storytelling by turn taking	* Facilitate/monitor interaction
			 * One speaker at a time
			 * Paraphrasing
			 * Open questions
			 * Encourage expression of feelings
				* Itinerate meetings
				 * "Peace" conference
					* Iterative inter-subclan deliberations (2-6 months)
					 * Multiple contacts/multiple groups
					 * Guurti/broad forum (2-6 months)
					 * Right to speak
					 * Cross-clan elders council
					 * Listen/moderate/arbitrate

3. Locate Conflict	* Where are we? * Identify core concerns * Create common meaning * Create a framework for advancing on concerns	* Identify issues	* Create list/agenda of issues * Reframe issues	* Surface issues * Legitimate grievances	* Poetry/proverb to provide frame/meaning * Lengthy orations
4. Arrange/Negotiate	* How do we get out? * Address nature of relationship * Seek solution to issues/concerns * Create paths toward resolution/reconciliation	* Problem solving on issues * Healing/relational focus	* One issue at a time * Separate interest/positions * Generate options * Narrow to mutual solutions	* Open forum * Coalition building behind scenes	* Qu'at sessions * Iterative inter-subclan deliberations * Deals on past grievances (Restitution) * Future relations
5. Way out/Agreement	* Who does what, when? * How will relationships continue * Monitor/implementation	* Agreements	* Written * Concise/clear * Reality test * Follow-up contact	* Agreements	* Written/oral * Exchange of camels/women for marriage * Establish councils/monitoring mechanism

Figure 11

Third-Party Involvement in Social Conflict

with the conflict will be constructed. In general, in one way or another, what is sought is a mechanism to bring to the surface and seek remedy for the problem. The third party, in this sense, provides a way to seek help. Involved is not only an initial negotiation of the proper place to lodge the conflict, but also a definition of the expectations for the roles and process that will be followed.

Gathering Perspectives, or what is often referred to as storytelling, responds to the question of "what happened?" In other words, it opens a space for looking at the past, providing opportunity for people to express and air their grievances and concerns. Important and widely shared needs in social conflict include the process of legitimation of concern through acknowledgement of pain and feelings, past wrongs and grievances, truth, and responsibilities. Perhaps most crucial is the element of legitimating a recognition and acknowledgment of the person or groups involved, in other words, being heard and taken seriously.

Locating the Conflict grapples with the question "where are we?" often metaphorically referred to by people in conflict who are trying to figure out where they are in relationship to others and problems experienced. It is the process of attaching meaning to events and people's action and situating what the conflict is about in order to know how to deal with it. This is the fundamental need to create an understanding of the conflict and a common framework that permits people to move forward.

Arrange and Negotiate answer the dilemma of "how do we get out?" Here the focus is on dealing with the nature of the relationship and the issues posed by the conflict. "Arranging" points toward a broader process of how the relationship is understood by the those in conflict. Negotiate deals with the narrower focus of how issues will be resolved, at times referred to as problemsolving. In the end, the process will help create paths leading toward resolution of some aspects of the conflict and redefinition of the relationship.

Way Out and Agreement deal with the questions of "who will do what, when?" Agreement tends to be more specific in terms of concrete expected action and implementation. The way out, on the other hand, points toward the broader mechanism that acknowledges ongoing ebb and flow of conflict in the context of relationship. In other words, it points, metaphorically, toward conflict as part of relational journey, where paths may cross, broaden together, or part their ways.

The form-formula columns outline the increasingly more specific ways that the facets and functions are met in particular settings and situations. For the purposes of demonstrating the application of the tool, I have suggested in figure 11 two broad comparisons of form and formula emerging from radically different settings. The first is the approach that might commonly be used in community mediation in the United States; the second outlines some aspects of how conflicts have been handled in elders conferences in the Somali context. In brief narrative, and not assuming any attempt here to be comprehensive in either process, we could suggest the following:

In the community mediation approach, the general form for entry involves a formal mediator role, often a person who is trained as a volunteer, or in some instances views himself or herself as a professional. By formalization, I refer to the explicit, often written understanding of the role and expectations. The process is more often than not oriented toward providing face-to-face encounters between the disputants and facilitated by the mediator.

The entries under formula are more specific. Disputants contact a center. They are brought into a process aimed at gaining acceptance for meeting in a facilitated session. The session itself is governed by ground rules and takes place at a neutral location, often the mediation center itself. Sessions are conceived as blocks of time—usually two hours or less—and may be carried out in multiple meetings over several weeks to several months depending on the complexity of the case. A key in the development of the mediator role and early process are the mechanisms for creating trust and a safe atmosphere for the disputants.

Drawing from personal experience and the research of Dr. A. Y. Farah (1993) on Somali peace conferences in Northwest Somalia, currently declared Somaliland, we can describe some characteristics for dealing with inter-clan conflict. Generally, serious inter-clan conflict will call for the movement toward creating a *guurti* or a supreme council of elders. This involves a collective coordination over a considerable period of time, where elders are recognized as having traditional power for facilitating and arbitrating the process and events and monitoring the outcomes.

In the severely divided, war-torn context, the formula for entry involved among other things the use of delegations of women, who, by marriage, were now connected to one clan, but who could also safely travel back to their clans of origin to pass on communication and encourage the initiation of cross-clan dialogue. The same may be true of a delegation of recognized elders that travels to meet another subclan's elders, referred to traditionally as an *ergada*. These early contacts make way for a space where fighting is stopped while consultations emerge.

An open, multiple, and cross-clan peace conference is preceded often by a combination of intra-sub–subclan deliberations about grievances, issues and representation and then a series of iterant, cross-subclan deliberations and consultations. Iteration refers to a process whereby no one meeting or consultation is seen as conclusive, but remains open and ongoing over time. This consultative process is where perspectives are gathered, procedural steps are negotiated, and the basic parameters are set for moving toward a more explicit forum guided by the *guurti*. The preparatory phase may appear like a traveling (literally as in *itinerate*) set of inconclusive consultations. In fact, setting parameters, negotiating agenda, and establishing the beginnings of a reconciliation process are being conducted. What is described here meets the facets of entry, perspective gathering, and locating and arranging in a circular, iterative process. The process itself builds from smaller collectives toward a larger collective and forum—a bottom-up approach to peace building.

The actual forum or peace conference can take the form of large, usually public meetings, marked by lengthy oratory speeches and the extensive use of poetry. People present have a basic felt right to speak. As a Somali proverb puts it, "You can deny a Somali his food but not his word." Poetry remains a revered art form and can move people toward war or toward reconciliation. As a formula of conflict resolution it helps locate and situate grievances and meaning and justifies views and demands of different groups. It is a traditional mechanism that has modern parallel in the mass media's effect on public opinion and conflict analysis in terms of locating the conflict by arguing for causes, rights, and responsibilities.

Given these components, the preparation and the conduct of a peace conference can easily last four to six months. Throughout, the elders help prepare, moderate, listen, and, in a number of cases, arbitrate procedural problems, as well as helping formulate an eventual consensus of the clans on the substance and relationship. While the open meeting provides one forum, simultaneously, a variety of inter and subclan deliberations continue on the side, at times involving lengthy, late-night *qu'at* sessions. (*Qu'at* is a leaf traditionally chewed and used for facilitating talks.)

In the community mediation model, disputants are expected to reveal their concerns and feelings. The mediator's tasks are to provide an atmosphere for hearing and identifying the issues and to work on the relationship. This is accomplished, for example, by paraphrasing and posing open questions to get more information and by helping to identify a common agenda or list of issues to negotiate as the process moves toward problem solving.

In the movement toward negotiation and arranging, mediation has a series of common techniques. For example, mediators will ask disputants to focus on one issue at a time, to separate their proposed solutions from their underlying interests, and to brainstorm a variety of options before they evaluate and move toward a solution. Generally, the focus of mediation is to discover mutually beneficial solutions and outcomes.

As these come together in pieces or packages, the community mediation process recommends formulating them in a final agreement that is written, concise, and clear. It usually outlines specific detail around expected actions. Mediators serve as a reality check in terms of whether the proposed agreements can be accomplished. Often, some form of follow-up contact with the mediators is included in the final agreement as a mechanism for monitoring or assuring the implementation.

In the Somali context, the agreements initially achieved in an oral format have taken written form in the recent peace conferences (1992–94). They may involve specific and traditional mechanisms for dealing with cross-clan conflicts and restitution, for example, the payment of female camels as compensation. Past grievances and restoration of relationship have also traditionally been accomplished by the exchange of women for marriage between two warring clans—seen as both a symbolic compensation for the loss of life and a bond of blood connection between the groups (Farah 1993). In many instances, the elders and the elders councils continue to function as monitors and guarantors of the peace agreements.

Although brief and incomplete, the comparison provides an example of convergence in terms of universal/particular and prescriptive/elicitive. What I am suggesting is that training on third party roles and mediation can help participants recognize key needs and functions the process may serve. On the other hand, the training process must also recognize the limitations of given forms and formulas and seek to work with those that are more culturally rooted and adapted to the nature of the problem and the context within which it moves.

Facet/Function suggest the usefulness of prescriptive and universal perspectives. There are shared, common, and, in that way, transferable ideas and approaches that can be helpful and can cross-fertilize. Form/Formulas suggest the usefulness of elicitive and more particular cultural discovery work. There is a need to innovate, adapt, and work in appropriate ways in each and every setting. In the end, as trainers, we must be flexible to pull from both resources what is needed at a given time and for a given purpose in the training.

Conclusion

In this chapter, I have attempted to demonstrate the possibility of approaching training as the challenge of working together with a group to discover and develop a model of mediation. In a number of the examples, especially the Central American- and U.S.-based community mediation, it is important to note the difference between a more professional, formalized process and the informal, traditional mechanisms. The prescriptive and elicitive approaches are in part the distinction and comparison between the transfer of a formal, more professional model in one society, in this case the North American, and the more informal, folk model of another, as was described in the Central American model in figure 10. The question then arises of whether a similar folk model would emerge if an elicitive approach were to be applied in the North American setting. And whether, therefore, we are comparing apples and oranges. In other words, we may not be dealing exclusively with cultural differences between countries and societies, but rather with cultural differences between educational levels and economic classes within the same society.

This concern is not new to the research in some regards. In fact, the empirical work by Merry and Silbey (1984) suggested that the models of community mediation tested in the Northeastern United States, having developed in formal training under the heavy influence of what they regard as Western academic concern for rational analysis and problem solving, did not fit the modalities of more working-class constituencies, who were looking for different approaches in seeking remedy.

What I am proposing here is not that the one intervention model is better than another. Rather, I am pushing for the expansion of how we approach the training methodology to include the process of discovery of how people actually think and go about seeking remedy and solution and how that knowledge can be tapped as a resource and foundation for developing models that fit clearly in a given setting.

In sum, an elicitive orientation suggests that we consider what is present in a cultural setting the basis for identifying key categories and concepts to use as foundational building blocks for a conflict resolution model. It assumes that the culture is a resource and that participants are capable of identifying and naming their own realities and tools. Practically, this means they dig into the mines of their own knowledge and setting. Rather than learning the language of a new model (for example, the North American mediation language about information gathering, assessment, and problem solving), and then needing to ferret out the implicit assumptions from that model for a particular cultural context, the elicitive approach initiates learning with the implicit but constructive images and assumptions present in the culture and builds toward an explicit model. It is therefore necessary for us to have available a pure elicitive approach in contrast with a pure prescriptive approach, in order to find the ways that these provide orientation, options, and convergence in terms of training methodology.

10

Role Plays
Tools for Discovery and Creation

Role plays and simulations are a major part of conflict-resolution training, and particularly so in mediation. Most often they are used to practice a given skill, learn an overall process, or work on specific kinds of situations mediators may face. In almost all of those circumstances, the trainer prepares the simulation ahead of time, often with detailed instructions laying out the various perspectives and situational circumstances. In experimenting with an elicitive approach to training, I have approached role-play as a means for model discovery and creation rather than exclusively model practice. This approach requires a shift in thinking not only about "role plays" but about the use and purpose of training time generally, about our willingness as trainers to trust the participant's own creative abilities. It involves the risk of not preparing role plays prior to the training, opting for a process where participants identify and create their own in the course of the event. Although I consistently set up the first steps of creating role plays in a similar fashion, there are numerous ways to use them once identified. I will outline the setup and several of the variations providing a rationale and purpose for each.

Setting Up for Role-Play Creation

Participants are divided into small groups. Each person is asked to think about and then describe to their group a conflictive situation that they have been aware of, have witnessed, or in which they were active participants. They are given a wide latitude; however, I find it preferable if they think about conflictive situations that are familiar to their immediate setting and experience. This step can be accomplished in about an hour, although one should not downplay the potential learning and effort to describe a conflictive situation and even the therapeutic aspect of sharing with others the elements of personal experience.

Having heard and talked about the various situations, the group is asked to choose one of the cases to present back to the larger group. The criteria for choosing include situations that would be interesting for the rest of the group to work with and that may be particularly challenging or relevant at this time, situations that represent typical patterns or problems, or situations that lend themselves to dramatization with clearly identified parts to be played.

The groups are asked to report back to a plenary session. Each group is asked to present a brief description of its chosen situation giving it a name like, "The case of the jealous husband."

Typically, with a group of thirty people the overall process takes between two and three hours, depending on the level of detail that is desired as cases are presented. Notice that the setup encourages everyone to participate and assumes that everyone is a resource. People begin to focus in on real-life events and situations. Thus, the scenarios that emerge are rooted in the kinds of problems and challenges they face in their context. There is also a level of community and solidarity that is fostered as people share from their experiences and begin to recognize their commonalities and initiate the task of naming their problems and obstacles.

At a practical level, the immediate outcome of the process is to provide the group with a reserve of six to ten role plays, depending on the number of small groups. These role plays often vary widely in terms of the kind of situations identified and can be drawn on during the rest of the training for the various aspects of work the group may want to concentrate on. There are now numerous directions the group could go with these situations, depending on the purpose and time available. I will describe several typical variations that I have used.

Stage the Conflict

The first is for people to stage the conflict. The small group that proposed this particular situation is asked to set it up and dramatize some aspect of it for the group. The group is given complete freedom to draw on other participants and to create the setting, the roles, the attitudes, and the relevant issues. As the small group is setting up to role-play, I pay careful attention to their preparatory discussion. This is not lost time, but in fact is a window into people's implicit, taken-for-granted knowledge about conflict in their setting and how it operates. Constructing the role play is a recreation of their realities, of what they know about their setting, their people and how things work. As a trainer, I am interested not only in the way they set up the conflict but also the language used to describe events, people, attitudes, and issues. If possible these can be jotted down on newsprint or a blackboard—making explicit potential categories and dynamics in conflict but with reference to their natural language.

The role play is then enacted for the rest of the group, in many cases producing considerable enjoyment, laughter, and, at times, deep emotions from fear to tears. In the settings where I have had more experience with this process—Latin America and East Africa—I am consistently amazed at peoples' ability to create these experiences and how closely the results approximate real-life dynamics. Discussion among the full group is encouraged once the role play has been enacted. Again, careful attention to how people think and talk about the situations and dynamics is an important tool for identifying key understandings, obstacles they face, and ways that they approach these problems.

Introducing Third-Party Help

A second variation is the introduction of a third party into a role play. In this instance, several people are asked how they would approach this situation, if they have an interest in helping, or, as is sometimes the case when the small group describes its role play, if someone from within the situation has asked for help. Two steps in setting up this variation are crucial for highlighting an elicitive approach.

First, the "helpers" are given full freedom to decide how to approach this situation. I go as far as pushing out questions such as these: "In a real-life situation, if you were to enter this problem in a constructive way, who would you likely be? Where would you start? Whom would you meet with? Where would you meet? How would you approach them?"

Second, it is most instructive as a device for discovery if the role play is done in a fishbowl, where the rest of the group watches the choices and approaches the helpers have made. Although intervention in the role play can create a feeling of vulnerability for the helpers, and therefore is best done in groups that have developed a sense of trust with each other, such interaction fosters a much more dynamic and rich discussion about what happened, what worked, what did not, what is typical of the way we do things, and what things need to be worked on. It is often in this discussion that people begin to name key categories, obstacles, and even the process.

Reiterating, our goal at this stage is discovering and creating models. As a trainer, I have backed away from "demonstrating" a process. The choices I would make about whom to talk with first, whom to bring together, where we should meet, what pace of talk we would use, how I define the issues, and so forth, are all rooted in my experience and expertise in other settings. Rather, these choices are the very things that are useful for people in the setting itself to define.

Examples from Training Experiences

Let me illustrate this by returning to the example in chapter 4 of the role play where I inadvertently turned two Guatemalans into "gringos." Close evaluation of how that happened would suggest a number of subtle but crucial elements, virtually all present in the set up and control of the role play.

1. We were discussing a family matter involving a father and a daughter, but the way I arranged the seating, with the three of us in a triangle, it probably emulated office space. That setting cre-

ated an implicit formalization and professionalization of my role. Further, it was my space, not theirs; and, also important, it was indoors.

2. I started by addressing everyone equally, describing what we would do, and then immediately moving to their views of the problems. I assumed a number of things about family structure, age, and roles that were common to my setting not theirs.

3. The approach assumed that talking it out between the two principal protagonists was both possible and desirable. The people present in the role play were members of the same family, yet I did not include other immediate or extended family. The conflict was reduced to its interpersonal dimension, assuming a certain level of individual autonomy and limited kinship networking.

4. Posing open questions about what was going on and what were their views presented a rapid pace of direct talk and self-disclosure, where cognitive skills of analysis and issue identification are prominent. In other words, the format and structure of the process was direct and analytical, assuming a considerable level of trust.

In sum, these elements, typical of a North American mediation session, contributed to the transformation of the two Guatemalans into gringos.

Compare that process with how two Nicaraguans approached a situation identified by them. It involved a jealous, unemployed husband and a wife who had a job. She had been thrown out of the house and accused of "flirting," a situation identified by them in an earlier session.

1. They began by defining realistically what might provide them entry, rather than assuming a preconceived role. "Let's say we are married, and live in the neighborhood and the wives are close friends." Procedurally, they then suggested steps related to natural contact and networking of the wives and husbands.

2. The wives met as they went to market. The encounter went through considerable exchange about family, kids, the disastrous economic crunch, and the war and eventually made its way to the deep pain of the marital problems. Revelation came through trust and holistic connection. The wives concluded that maybe the husbands could talk.

3. The "helper" husband and wife talked about the situation.

4. The husband then looked for an opportunity to discuss this with his counterpart alone.

5. The role play continued with several separate encounters until several hours later when the two disputants were invited for a pig roast at the helpers' house, their first encounter since they had separated.

In the debriefing that followed, the discussion focused on the approach of meeting separately, how to prepare the way for reconciliation, how to approach husband/wife conflicts, how to use the natural family and neighborhood networks, and what to do with *machismo* and abusive relationships in a setting of economic poverty, low self-esteem, and war.

Conclusion

These latter two stories underscore the key points of this chapter and illustrate the promises and pitfalls of how role plays are used in the prescriptive and elicitive models.

In the *gringo* example, the role play emerged in a prescriptive framework and presented an explicit model of mediation with implicit cultural assumptions. Those implicit premises not only got in the way, but had a subtle, disempowering effect. The role play kept the Guatemalans from discovering and naming their own process by presuming their entry into a foreign process.

In the Nicaraguan example, carried out in more of an elicitive-oriented framework, the role play developed on implicit understandings emerging out of their setting, but did not yet represent an explicit model. The experience set the stage for identification, naming, and development of a model, but at its initial level remained as raw material. The process, rooted in culturally relevant knowledge, nudged the participants to seek resources and build on those in developing as peacemakers in their setting.

What is needed is a combination of the two. On the one hand, where an explicit model from one setting is presented in another, it is critical to examine and identify some of the implicit cultural assumptions on which it is built. On the other hand, where implicit understandings emerge, the trainer, either with model comparison or further group work, must help create the movement toward establishing an explicit model that can be described and practiced.

In conclusion, I am suggesting that role plays can be developed in the course of training and can serve as tools for building appropriate models for dealing with conflict. Although this elicitive role-play exercise may take additional time, it is rooted in the context and knowledge of participants. These are both relevant in discovering key cultural resources for building appropriate models targeted at felt needs. However, the process shifts the role of trainer from that of an expert in the mediation process to that of a facilitator sparking an encounter between participants and their own knowledge and creativity.

11

Facing Multicultural Settings

Throughout this section, I have concentrated on outlining the perspective and strategies of the elicitive model in training and how it may be applied within a cultural setting. For the most part, I have assumed working with participants who share a common language and cultural heritage. In the real world, however, such an assumption is not always possible or necessarily desirable. From the former Yugoslavia to Sri Lanka, from Nairobi to Toronto, conflicts are often rooted and expressed in and between multiethnic and multicultural settings and groups. The challenge for creative training is not simply a question of how to respect and understand a given cultural group, but how to do that within a setting where multiple groups are present and interdependent.

This reality begs three relevant questions related to an elicitive framework. First, is an elicitive strategy applicable in multicultural settings? Second, how is an elicitive-oriented approach relevant in settings populated with diverse communities in transition—who represent varying degrees of assimilation in the host culture and of displacement from their root setting—a reality that implies a mix of old and new values and social organization? Third, how is an elicitive strategy relevant in settings where people have experienced a process of urbanization and modernization that has removed or at least distanced them from their own traditional cultural values and modalities for dealing with conflict—often creating a vacuum between competing influences or at the very least between generations of the same group?

Each of these questions, and certainly any given setting where training may take place, merits a fuller and more specific exploration of the parameters and histories of the groups involved. I believe, however, it is possible to extrapolate from the elicitive frame of reference a number of broad suggestions applicable to multicultural and dynamically changing settings. We should take note that in many of these settings, current training has tended toward a "sensitive-prescriptive" approach by which a generic model of mediation is presented to the various cultural groups, encouraging them to interact with and then adapt the model to their needs. This is clearly preferable to an approach that outright suggests a model with little or no room for adaptation. But, the questions we raise here are whether we can expand to include elicitive modalities in training, what potential that training has, and how it would work in a multicultural context.

Guiding Principles

To answer these questions we must recognize that the core of the elicitive-oriented approach lies less with technique, than with a framework that attempts to integrate training methodology and goals, and with a reorientation in how the roles of trainer and participants are understood. The framework is built around a set of foundational principles that raise certain kinds of questions as one approaches a training event. We can reiterate and explore a number of these assumptions, principles, and questions in the context of a multicultural training.

The Principle of Conflict "In situ"

In situ refers to seeing something in its original position. In this context, I am referring to the very simple idea of looking at conflict and conflict resolution modalities in a given setting as present and functioning. In other words, through the in situ prin-

ciple, as a trainer, I assume that models for dealing with conflict
are present and practiced in some form in and between
multicultural groups living in any given situation.

In many settings where I have lived and worked, I have heard
people say, "This conflict resolution thing is new. It doesn't exist
here." What they mean is that formal, explicitly acknowledged,
and institutionalized modalities of alternative dispute resolution
do not exist outside of socially sanctioned mechanisms such as the
police or courts. I often reply by describing conflict resolution
through the metaphoric image of a river. In any given community, conflict exists, like rain. Into every life a little rain will fall.
The interesting in situ question is this. Where does the rain go?
Where do the tributaries and then the rivers of conflict run? I assume there is a river of conflict that leads somewhere. In other
words, in a given community, and even more importantly, in a
given cultural group within a multicultural community, including those more established and those that are very recent arrivals, conflict ends up on somebody's doorstep. Where and to whom
in a community does conflict flow?

The in situ principle raises two important points of inquiry
related to training in multicultural settings. First, it suggests a need
for an inquisitive mind about what exists and how people think
about and use their natural resources. A noninquisitive mind assumes a community without formal alternative dispute mechanisms is a vacuum to be filled with prepackaged products. Second,
it suggests that the starting point for training is not the event itself but rather it is the process of exploration and identification
of people, who are wet up to their ears, standing midstream in
the river of conflict from within each cultural group that makes
up a multicultural setting. This leads to the second principle.

The Principle of Indigenous Empowerment

This principle underscores that people from the setting are the
key resource in the training. What shifts in reflecting on how to
apply this principle in multicultural settings is the need to foster
a preparatory strategy that maximizes the potential resource they
represent.

An elicitive framework suggests that when approaching a multicultural setting, an explicit strategy should develop for identifying implicit but functioning conflict resolvers and peacemakers within each cultural group. This exploration must be based on a broad conception of handling conflict and looking for resources. In some instances, it may be the residue of an elder model where the oldest of the young arrivals play a significant role. In other cases it may be the local priest, or even the corner pub's bartender. The guiding questions remain: where do conflicts end up, who do people go to, and who feels responsible within a cultural community. The strategic aspect of this quest is to identify, validate, and empower these people and to create the opportunity for cross-fertilization and interaction with their counterparts in other communities.

This principle suggests that training is more than an event and the content shared in the course of the event. It must involve a serious strategic effort aimed at the empowerment of the cultural and ethnic resources available in a given setting by respecting and seeking first what is present and how it operates as the seedbed for creative innovation and development. Rather than attempting to train and get representation of a given cultural community into our mediation center, it suggests the nurturing of respectful relationships and seeking to understand the conflict and its modalities through the eyes of the communities as a key prerequisite for the long-term project of developing sustainable, cross-cultural models in the broader community.

The Principle of Conscientization

Conscientization is awareness-of-self-in-context. It seeks a catalyst that sparks and creates an encounter of people with themselves and with the realities they experience and face. Conscientization believes that people are knowledgeable about, capable of naming, interacting with, and responding to their own realities in dynamic ways. In regard to multicultural settings, this principle is based on several fundamental ideas.

First, the elicitive principle suggests that people in a community are capable of identifying and naming the realities of conflict they face. It assumes a process that fosters this reflection—probing the awareness of conflict and of self in context across the cultural or ethnic groups living within a community—will create opportunity for important insights and learning, as implicit, often taken-for-granted knowledge is shared at an explicit level. This knowledge is understood as the key resource for the training.

Second, it suggests that the most useful, transformative, and constructive critique of the problems, strengths, and weaknesses related to handling conflict within a given cultural group emerges from that group. This realization does not exclude outside insight, but does place primary emphasis on in-context resources.

Let me try to make this point in more detail given the multicultural and ethnic settings we are approaching in this chapter. In settings where cross-ethnic conflict is divisive and violent, people are often operating from a stance of preservation and defensiveness. Each group experiences a deep-rooted and deep-felt threat to its identity and well-being, often creating a sense of prevailing insecurity that we are not safe. Paradoxically, insecurity protects itself by lashing out at others who are the perceived threat but who, more often than not, are equally insecure, thus creating a mutually reinforcing and destructive cycle. Conscientization suggests a paradoxical approach to this cycle. It invites a particular group to reflect within itself on the strengths and weaknesses of its own heritage, knowledge, and modalities related to conflict— in contrast to reflecting on the threat or modalities of others or adopting a posture that members must initially learn from others because they have no resources. By so doing, group members become their own best critics, moving toward a proactive rather than a reactive posture and simultaneously strengthening the respect for their own identity, a key component in breaking out of the vicious cycle.

The Principle of "Recycling"

This principle is aimed at the key question of how to work with groups that have or are experiencing significant cultural change and transition. For example, in African settings, particularly urban ones, people talk of the dilemma created in large part by modernization, urbanization, and Western education in which significant portions of the population no longer rely on traditional ways of social organization and specifically handling conflict, on the one hand, nor do modern Western models fulfill their needs, on the other. In many European and North American metropolitan areas, the refugee and recent migrant communities find themselves in the process of acculturation where the social resources for handling conflict in their home setting are no longer available in the host context, yet the new situation does not adequately deal with these needs.

In these situations, the principle of recycling is applicable. To draw the root metaphor, recycling is a dynamic process that mixes "old, used things" with the fresh ingredients to recreate a new product. We note that it neither discards the old nor embraces with blind faith the perpetually replaceable new as the answer to our needs. In practical terms, recycling invites people to reflect back on what existed, on what was known from within their context, and to identify what is missing in the current context. This review represents a constructively critical and innovative process of reflection that permits a particular cultural group to identify the strengths of its own heritage but also to face the realities of current demands.

The Principle of Facilitation

This principle suggests that trainers working in multicultural settings assume a posture of leadership that is closer to a facilitator of group process than of an expert in a particular model of conflict resolution. This shift lies at the heart of the elicitive process and is particularly applicable in multicultural training settings.

The trainer-as-facilitator envisions the overall training group as made up of unique individual cultural and ethnic groups, more like a garden salad than a melting pot. Each has valid and important insights and knowledge about the problem, the possible options, the mechanisms and resources their particular community has or needs, and the viability of proposed solutions. The purpose of the training is to validate and draw on these insights and knowledge and to use them in the creation of cooperative conflict resolution models in the setting. Thus, rather than seeing the various groups within a multicultural setting as target groups who receive training from an expert in a generic, shared model, the trainer understands the role as the facilitation of a dynamic process that catalyzes discovery and model creation as the key.

Outlining a Multicultural Training Event

The elicitive-oriented approach in multicultural settings can be fleshed out by considering how these principles could be applied in practice. For our purposes here, let us assume we are working in the context of a training event that brings together a number of culturally diverse groups living in a common urban setting. To make it manageable, we will suggest that four groups have been identified (for example, African American, Salvadoran, Korean, and Anglo-American), and from each, eight to ten key leaders were chosen from the various communities. To make it more realistic, let us assume that these communities live in encroaching geographic proximity and have experienced recent and escalating tensions. A possible elicitive approach might follow these steps in the course of a three-day workshop.

1. After plenary overview and introductions, as a first step, each group is asked to meet separately for the first work session (one and one-half hours). In each group, each individual is asked to describe a real-life conflict either witnessed or participated in recently. Depending on the overall purpose and longer-term time frame of the training event, people are encouraged to focus on a particular area or more broadly. For our purposes, we will suggest they focus on cross-cultural or ethnic situations. The group must choose two of the situations to describe in detail in the plenary session, at least one of which it feels will lend itself well to a role-play format.

2. In the plenary session, a spokesperson from each group is asked initially to describe the two situations. In the functional role of facilitation, the trainers push out with the group the nature and development of the cases, paying special attention to the language and categories used to describe the situation. The purpose at this stage is not merely to hear the facts, but rather to begin the process of exploring a particular group's insight and knowledge about

conflict as a window into how this situation is understood and experienced. When all the groups have reported, an overview summary from the trainers could suggest some commonalities in themes and types of situations. These cases, likely numbering between five and eight depending on overlap, are now the raw material for the rest of the seminar. This process has taken a full morning.

3. Assuming that the purpose of the training is to develop appropriate intervention models in cross-cultural settings, one of the cases is now chosen as a starting point. Volunteer participants are drawn from the various groups to take roles described in the situation, representing wherever possible their own cultural group in the roles assigned (for example, Salvadorans are chosen to play Salvadoran roles in the role play). These people, in collaboration with the trainers, are asked to prepare their roles and the details of the situation creating a common story of events.

Parallel to the role-play preparation, each cultural group meets separately to discuss how it would approach this particular situation in order to intervene constructively in its resolution. Members are given an open-ended assignment starting from ground zero. They must decide, for example, at what point they would initiate the intervention, whom they would approach and in what order, who they would need to be in order to approach these people, where they would approach them, with what style and pace, and so on.

Having now devised a strategy, one group is given the opportunity to play out that approach directly with the role players in a fish-bowl format where others will observe. An initial negotiation with the role players indicates at what point in the conflict they wish to intervene and with whom they wish to meet. Following that, the intervening group may decide its steps and process. The role players are asked to take the perspective of a person whom they are representing from their own culture and respond to the intervention initiative as naturally as possible. If, for example, the intervening group brings them together for a face-to-face meeting and they do not feel comfortable with direct confrontation, they should indicate that through their natural cultural mechanisms, even if it is not picked up by others.

Following the fish-bowl role play, the trainer-facilitator debriefs the interaction. The primary purpose (reiterated a number of times throughout) is not whether the case was resolved, but rather the thinking, intention, and implicit model under which the group pursued the intervention. The trainer-facilitator moves carefully back and forth during the debriefing between various groups and the resources they represent. From the group who devised the strategy, careful thought is given to identifying and naming the cultural categories and strategies that emerge for handling conflict and working as a third party, permitting people to reflect and constructively critique their own cultural resources and gaps. From other groups, particularly role players, the impact of the approach can be discussed in terms of how they experienced it from within their cultural framework. A special effort is made to summarize initial ideas and strategies after each debriefing. This process, using one case study, would likely take a full afternoon schedule. With a different or even the same case, the process could be repeated but inviting a different group to develop their strategy in the fish bowl.

4. A next step would invite participants to link and develop approaches that draw from the various learnings and models that were identified. In this step, a role play would be chosen and players would be identified. However, the intervention would be developed by multicultural teams—each devising a strategy for approaching the particular situation.

Conclusion

Multicultural settings represent an enormous challenge requiring insight, sensitivity, and creativity. In this chapter, I have suggested that the elicitive-oriented approach is applicable to such settings, not so much in terms of a specific content, but rather in terms of its general orientation based on an alternative way of thinking about training. This approach involves seeing training as a process, the trainer as a facilitator, and the participants as resourceful people capable of discovering and creating models of intervention rooted in their context. Perhaps most crucial is the idea of training as a process based on relationship building and not an event. In this regard, the goal then becomes the development of networks and linkages that can be sustained over time through the training within and between the various participating communities. Such an orientation does not proceed on the basis of teaching everyone a common model, but rather attempts to identify and then coordinate the cultural resources that exist within the communities in a given place.

12

Conclusions

Throughout this essay, I have developed the case for a constructive reconsideration of how we approach training as we work with conflict across and in diverse cultural settings. The purposes were to both apply a more rigorous analysis to how, what, and why we "train" and to broaden the parameters of how we think about conflict, cultural resources, and transformation. Rather than returning to a broad summary of the key points as a conclusion, I prefer to reemphasize the heart of the argument and to push out several questions that remain unanswered. I think the key elements of my argument can be summarized in three points.

First, I have argued that the training project must be understood and integrated coherently into an overall peace-building framework, oriented toward social empowerment and change. I believe we accomplish that to the degree that we are explicit about the integration of ultimate objectives and strategic mechanisms for pursuing the goals. In other words, we should not operate on the supposed, self-evident basis that conflict resolution, as we understand it in North America, is good thing worthy of wide dissemination. We must also pay critical attention to the modalities, methodologies, and content of training and how each promotes the goals we espouse. I further suggest that this critical attention is all the more important as we cross cultural, ethnic, and class lines.

Second, I have suggested that an important, perhaps key aspect of training across cultures lies in the nature of the relationship between trainer and participant, at both conceptual and practical levels. The prescriptive/elicitive comparison underscores a movement away from or toward either a relationship that rests primarily on transfer of trainer expertise or one that promotes participatory discovery and creation rooted in cultural knowledge. I have argued that the key is not choosing between one or the other, but rather the expansion of the trainer repertoire to make both possible and therefore appropriate to the variety of settings and groups we trainers engage.

Third, I have argued that "culture" should not be understood by conflict resolvers and trainers primarily as a challenge to be mastered and overcome through technical recipes. Culture is rooted in social knowledge and represents a vast resource, a rich seedbed for producing a multitude of approaches and models in dealing with conflict. If approached as a seedbed, culture can be excited, probed, and fed. In more concrete terms, I have argued that training across and in other cultures should seek methodologies that create an encounter between people in a given setting and their own rich but often implicit understandings about conflict and how to handle it. I am advocating a proactive shift that suggests a people's accumulated and implicit knowledge is an extraordinary resource for developing appropriate conflict strategies within their setting. I have further suggested that this shift is not only methodologically possible, but that it promotes creativity and empowerment.

The question that remains, from the perspective of the arguments put forward in this essay, is how to combine the resources and potentiality of the training modalities.

First, I have presented the prescriptive/elicitive comparison as a spectrum. Either training model in its pure, extreme form is rarely useful. In practical terms, in my own experience and experiments, I have found that training events in conflict resolution are often a mix of the two. The comparative spectrum helps identify the crucial tension between these orientations and the potential for a more comprehensive training repertoire. In turn, this identification permits us to reflect critically on both our purposes and methodologies related to training, not just on our techniques. In other words, it is not my intention to eliminate, or minimize the expertise that a given trainer may have accumulated, which is indeed an enormous resource for training. However, I do believe it is legitimate to question the social value attached to that explicit expertise and the modalities for its delivery in a given relationship, especially if that expertise supersedes or undermines the cultural resources within a given setting. Identifying the full spectrum of possibilities helps us recognize the limitations and premises of a prescriptive model of training too often taken for granted. As such, the prescriptive-elicitive spectrum provides a tool for examining our assumptions about universality of conflict-resolution practices and appropriately suggests that transferability is understood as an explicit strategic choice among a variety of possible vehicles useful for preparing people for peace-building activity.

With this as backdrop, I make the second observation that prescriptive and elicitive approaches can be combined in cross-cultural training when understood in the context and relationship of interaction rather than transfer. By this statement, I mean the following. When conflict resolution models from one setting are promoted in another, it is incumbent on the trainers to be explicit about the cultural boundedness of the model. I believe this can happen through several important mechanisms.

First, the trainers should do their homework in becoming aware and recognizing the cultural assumptions implicit in their model. These should be explicitly identified with the participants. I do not believe it is sufficient for trainers to say: "This is a North American model of mediation. It may or may not be applicable here." I am suggesting that we, as trainers from any setting, have the further responsibility of identifying more explicitly the cultural and contextual assumptions that make up a given model we may present.

Second, an interactive rather than transfer environment can be structurally established in the training by openly including exploration into the participants' knowledge, cultural heritage, and understanding of conflict in their context. Where outside models are introduced, participants should be explicitly invited to critique, argue with, change, and outright reject the proposed model from the standpoint of their setting and culture, as an integral and not a haphazard part of the training. I believe this helps create a legitimate respect for culture and mutual respect in relationships.

As a final word, I would say that the elicitive-oriented approach brings a certain set of lenses that affect how we see things in regard to culture, conflict, and training. These lenses are not a new layer of technique. They represent a different way of looking at and looking for resources in training and intervention in the conflict transformation adventure.

Bibliography
Index

Bibliography

Augsburger, David. 1986. *Pastoral Counseling Across Cultures*. Philadelphia: Westminster Press.

———. 1991. *Intercultural Mediation*. Philadelphia: Westminster Press.

Berger, Peter, and Thomas Luckman. 1967. *The Social Construction of Reality*. New York: Anchor Books.

Blumer, Herbert. 1969. *Symbolic Interactionism: Perspective and Method*. Englewood Cliffs, N.J.: Prentice Hall.

Boulding, Kenneth. 1962. *Conflict and Defense*. New York: Harper and Row.

Chupp, Mark. 1991. "When Mediation Is Not Enough." In *Conciliation Quarterly* 10, no. 3 (Summer): 4–6.

Cohen, Raymond. 1990. *Culture and Conflict in Egypt-Israeli Relations*. Bloomington: Indiana Univ. Press.

———. 1991. *Negotiating Across Cultures: Communication Obstacles in International Diplomacy*. Washington D.C.: United States Institute of Peace.

Coleman, James. 1956. *Community Conflict*. New York: Free Press.

Coser, Lewis. 1956. *The Functions of Social Conflict*. New York: Free Press.

Curle, Adam. 1971. *Making Peace*. London: Tavistock Publications.

———. 1991. *Tools for Transformation*. London: Hawthorne Press.

Dator, James. 1991. "Culturally Appropriate Dispute Resolution Techniques and the Formal Judicial System in Hawaii." A report to the Hon. Herman Lum, Chief Justice, Hawaii State Judiciary. Honolulu: Univ. of Hawaii.

Duryea, Michelle Lebaron. 1992. *Conflict and Culture: A Literature Review and Bibliography.* Vancouver: UVIC Institute of Dispute Resolution.

Farah, Ahmed Yusef. 1993. "The Roots of Reconciliation." London: Action Aid.

Fisher, Glen. 1980. *International Negotiation: A Cross Cultural Perspective.* Chicago: Intercultural Press.

Fisher, Roger, and William Ury. 1981. *Getting to Yes.* Boston: Houghton Mifflin.

Folberg, Jay, and Alison Taylor. 1984. *Mediation.* San Francisco: Jossey-Bass.

Freire, Paulo. 1970. *Pedagogy of the Oppressed.* New York: Seabury Press.

Friedman, Edwin. 1985. *Generation to Generation.* New York: Guilford Press.

———. 1990. *Friedman's Fables.* New York: Guilford Press.

Geertz, Clifford. 1983. "Thick Description: Toward an Interpretive Theory of Culture." In *Contemporary Field Research,* ed. R. Emerson, 37–59. Boston: Little, Brown.

Gulliver, P. H. 1979. *Disputes and Negotiations: A Cross-Cultural Perspective.* New York: Academic Press.

Hocker, Joyce, and William Wilmot. 1991. *Interpersonal Conflict.* Dubuque. Iowa: William C. Brown.

Hope, Anne, and Sally Timmel. 1988. *Training for Transformation.* Zimbabwe: Mambo Press.

Iklé, Fred C. 1964. *How Nations Negotiate.* New York: Harper and Row.

Kavanaugh, Jim. 1989. *Nunca decir no podemos: Una guía para la capacitación social.* San Jose, Costa Rica: Ministry of Justice.

Kelman, Herbert. 1965. *International Behavior: A Social-Psychological Analysis.* New York: Holt, Rinehart, and Winston.

Kriesberg, Louis, Terrell Northrup, and Stuart Thorson, eds. 1989. *Intractable Conflicts and Their Transformation.* Syracuse: Syracuse Univ. Press.

Kraybill, Ron, John Paul Lederach, and Alice Price. 1989. *Mediation Training Manual.* Akron, Pa.: Mennonite Central Committee.

Lakoff, George, and Mark Johnson. 1980. *Metaphors We Live By.* Chicago: Univ. of Chicago Press.

Lederach, John Paul. 1985. "Mediation in North America: An examination of the profession's cultural assumptions." Paper presented at the National Conference on Peacemaking and Conflict Resolution. Denver, Colo.

———. 1986. *La Regulación del Conflicto Social.* Akron, Pa.: Mennonite Central Committee.

———. 1988. "Of Nets, Nails, and Problemas." Ph.D. diss., Univ. of Colorado.

LeResche, Dianne. 1990. "Procedural Justice of, by, and for American Ethnic. Groups: A Comparison of Conflict Resolution Procedures Used
by Korean-Americans and American Community Mediation Centers
with Procedural Justice Theories." Ph.D. diss., George Mason Univ.

LeResche, Dianne, and Jennifer Spruill. 1991. "Training on Culture: A Survey of the Field." *Conciliation Quarterly* 9, no. 1: 2–5.

Marins, José, Teolide M. Trevisan, and Carolee Chanona. 1988. *Dinámicas.*
Mexico City: Centro de Reflexión Teológico.

McLellan, David. 1977. *Karl Marx: Selected Writings.* Oxford: Oxford Univ.
Press.

Merry, Sally, and Susan Silbey. 1984. "What do plaintiffs want? Re-
examining the Concept of Dispute." *The Justice System Journal* 9, no.
2:151–78.

Merry, Sally, and Neal Milner, eds. 1993. *The Possibility of Popular Justice.*
Ann Arbor: Univ. of Michigan Press.

Moore, Christopher. 1986. *Mediation.* San Francisco: Jossey-Bass.

Nader, Laura. 1990. *Harmony, Ideology, Justice, and Control in Sapotic Moun-
tain Village.* Stanford: Stanford Univ. Press.

———. 1993. "When is Popular Justice Popular?" In *The Possibility of Popular Justice,* ed. Sally Merry and Neal Milner, 435–54. Ann Arbor: Univ.
of Michigan Press.

Nader, Laura, and Harry F. Todd, eds. 1978. *The Disputing Process—Law
in Ten Societies.* New York: Columbia Univ. Press.

O'Brien, Niall. 1987. *Revolution from the Heart.* New York: Oxford Univ.
Press.

Richards, Paul. 1985. *Indigenous Agricultural Revolution.* Boulder, Colo.:
Westview Press.

Ruppesinghe, Kumar. 1994. *Protracted Conflict.* London: McMillan (in
press).

Samatar, Said. 1982. *Oral Poetry and Somali Nationalism.* Cambridge: Cambridge Univ. Press.

Schiere, Jacob. 1991. "Beyond Technology." An MCC Occasional Paper.
no. 14. Akron, Pa.: Mennonite Central Committee.

Schutz, Alfred. 1967. *The Phenomenology of the Social World.* Chicago:
Northwestern Univ. Press.

———. 1971. *Collected Papers Volume 1: The Problem of Social Reality.* The
Hague: Martinus Nijhoff.

Seidman, Ann, and Anang Frederick. 1992. *Towards a New Vision of Self-
Sustained Development.* Trenton, N.J.: Africa World Press.

Simmel, Georg. 1955. *Conflict and the Web of Group Affiliation.* New York:
The Free Press.

Smith, Kenwyn K., and David N. Berg. 1987. *Paradoxes of Group Life*. San Francisco: Jossey-Bass.

Spradley, James. 1979. *The Ethnographic Interview*. New York: Holt, Rinehart, and Winston.

Thomas, Kenneth. 1976. "Conflict and Conflict Management." In *Handbook of Industrial and Organizational Psychology*, ed. M. D. Dunnette, 120–46. Chicago: Rand McNally.

Volkan, Vamik, Demetrios Julius, and Joseph Montville. 1990. *The Psychodynamics of International Relations*. Lexington, Mass.: Lexington Books.

Walters, MariAnne, Betty Carter, Peggy Papp, and Olga Silverstein. 1988. *The Invisible Web: Gender Patterns in Family Relationships*. New York: Guilford Press.

Watzlawick, P., J. Weakland, and Richard Fisch. 1978. *Change*. New York: W. W. Norton.

Weber, Max. 1947. *The Theory of Social and Economic Organization*. New York: Oxford Univ. Press.

Wehr, Paul. 1979. *Conflict Regulation*. Boulder, Colo.: Westview Press.

Index

Page numbers in *italics* denote figures.

Syracuse Studies on Peace and Conflict Resolution
Harriet Hyman Alonso, Charles Chatfield, and Louis Kriesberg, *Series Editors*

A series devoted to readable books on the history of peace movements, the lives of peace advocates, and the search for ways to mitigate conflict, both domestic and international. At a time when profound and exciting political and social developments are happening around the world, this series seeks to stimulate a wider awareness and appreciation of the search for peaceful resolution to strife in all its forms and to promote linkages among theorists, practitioners, social scientists, and humanists engaged in this work throughout the world.

Other titles in the series include: